GRANT TEXTBOOK SERIES

VOLUME I
ELEMENTARY ASTROLOGY

CATHARINE T. GRANT
AND
ERNEST A. GRANT

Copyright 2020 by American Federation of Astrologers, Inc. All rights reserved.

No part of this book may be reproduced or transcribed in any form or by any means, electronic or mechanical, including photocopying or recording or by any information storage and retrieval system without written permission from the author and publisher, except in the case of brief quotations embodied in critical reviews and articles. Requests and inquiries may be mailed to: American Federation of Astrologers, Inc., 6535 S. Rural Road, Tempe, AZ 85283.

ISBN-13: 978-0-86690-676-0

Cover Design: Jack Cipolla

Published by:

American Federation of Astrologers, Inc.

6535 S. Rural Road

Tempe, AZ 85283

Contents

Chapter 1: Historical Perspective — 1

Chapter 2: Houses of the Horoscope — 24

Chapter 3: Signs of the Zodiac — 40

Chapter 4: Celestial Bodies — 54

Chapter 5: Calculating the Horoscope — 62

Chapter 6: Other Factors in Horoscope Erection — 94

Chapter 7: Alternate Methods of Horoscope Erection — 114

Chapter 8: Aspects — 125

Chapter 9: Sensitive Points — 135

References — 142

| Chapter 1 |

Historical Perspective

A HISTORY OF ASTROLOGY WOULD FILL many volumes, so the sole purpose of the following panoramic survey is to help the student realize that he or she is studying one of mankind's most fascinating sciences as well as its oldest.

As archaeological research penetrates the mists of antiquity and brings back the knowledge of the ancients, it also pushes the birthdate of astrology further into the past. At present, we can be certain only that it was a well-developed science by the earliest date of recorded history. Astrology even predates written records, as Hindu astrology was passed down by word of mouth for several centuries before the dawn of the Christian era.

The Chinese tri-grams of Fu-Hi, which are mankind's earliest graphic records (believed to antedate Christianity by 20,000 years) are astrological in nature and indicate that even then astrology was a well-defined science in China. Astrologer Ruth Hale Oliver places the discovery of the solar zodiac in Mesopotamia at about 8000 BC with the year beginning at the Winter Solstice on December 21 instead of, at present, the Vernal Equinox on March 21. Orientalist Jules Oppert found that Babylonian astrologers could have known certain astrological facts only by observing the fixed star Sirius from the island of Zylos in the Persian Gulf on April 29, 11542 BC.

Careful study of the Hebrew scriptures indicates active use of astrology by the Jewish people. Flavius Josephus, a Jewish historian of the first century AD, recorded the legend that Seth and his children were the inventors of astrology, and recorded the future predictions of Adam, which came through the Archangel Michael, on two pillars which would withstand flood and fire.[1] Josephus further pointed out that the patriarch Abraham took his information about astrology from Chaldea to Canaan when he resettled. Abraham was called a "man skillful in the celestial science."[2] The great geographer and historian Strabo, recorded (c AD 15) that in his day "A settlement is put apart for the local philosophers called Chaldeans, who are chiefly devoted to the study of astronomia. Some, not approved by the rest, profess to understand genethliology or the casting of nativities."[3]

Sir Isaac Newton pointed out the scientific use of astrology by the first Egyptian dynasties (long before this was confirmed by the archeologists) quoting from Diodorus Siculus (AD 59), "They say that the Chaldeans in Babylon, being colonies of the Egyptians, became famous for astrology, having learned it from the Egyptians."[4] While we know that Newton and Diodorus erred in their chronology, Chaldean astrology is believed to antedate that of Egypt, although some ancient Arabic astrological terms have been found to have a much earlier Egyptian root. The tablets of Sargon I of Agadi, who lived about 3800 BC, clearly prove the Chaldeans to have been competent astrologers by that period. According to Issac Meyer, a leading archaeologist of Chaldean and the pre-Chaldean empire of Akkadia, celestial observations in the latter date back to at least 4310 BC.

J. M. Thoburn, lecturer in philosophy at the University of Wales, has written: "So far as astrology goes, when we come to the principles, we reach the profoundest things in our experience. It is the principles, really, that were enunciated by the founders of astrology, at the beginning of human culture, or perhaps at the stage where the primal imagination of our race was just passing into, but had not quite reached, anything that could be called knowledge, intelligence, humanity, or culture. It is a startling but significant fact that this original enunciation of the principles has survived, more than any other creation of the human mind, the test of history."

Eventually, it will probably be found that astrology was not founded by one people but by many branches of the human family simultaneously as they progressed from savagery to the civilized state of logical reasoning and development. In support of this theory, the earliest records of China, India, Chaldea, Egypt, Mexico, South America, the Southwestern American cliff dwellers, and other peoples of antiquity scattered over the surface of the earth contain the remnants of an astrological science developed in proportion to the overall intellectual development of these peoples.

Thus astrology, together with religion, forms the oldest of all the sciences known to man. When an omnipotent creator sent the universe, with its myriad of twinkling stars, hurtling into space, two unvarying laws came into being.

The first: a desire on the part of man to *know*. The second: the immutable law which holds all matter together and keeps the universe in perfect *balance*. This law of balance has been expounded in the philosophies and religions of the ancients, by Moses and the Jewish prophets, and later by countless multitudes who followed these early beginnings of inspired enlightenment. As the intellect and faith of man increases, a true understanding of these laws and their interpretation will also increase.

The childish ditty, 'Twinkle, twinkle little star, how I wonder what you are," symbolizes man's desire to know the meaning of the universe – a desire that has been present in every generation. At an early date in man's intellectual life, the Sun by day, with the Moon and stars by night, challenged him to find a reason for the universe.

Mankind probably passed from a savage state to a pastoral state at the same time in different parts of the earth. As shepherds wandered to and fro, following their flocks through the long nights, it is reasonable to suppose that they observed the Moon and stars follow certain definite courses through the heavens, and the Sun to change its position with the seasons. Later they learned to plot these movements and noted that certain effects were produced when they reached points in the sky relative to each other and to points on the earth. Whether or not this is the true picture of the early development of astrology, certainly it did develop during this pastoral age. The shepherds became the Wise Men; they were sought out by persons desiring knowledge and the calling was one of high repute. Witness the Wise Men of the East *following* the star to the shepherds in the fields of Bethlehem.

Since the stars and the heavens were beyond their intellectual grasp, men associated the Sun, Moon, and planets with their religious beliefs or structured their religious doctrines around these celestial phenomena. Thus astrology became the science of the priests, particularly in Chaldea and Egypt. Evidence of this is seen in the astronomical and astrological (synonymous in those days) significance of the pyramids and of the worship of Bel, Ra, Amen–Ra, and Osiris.

In early Egypt, where black and white magic became highly developed, astrology by its very nature became associated with the former. However, there is nothing magic about astrology, nothing occult. It is purely an experimental science from which certain factual information has been developed through the centuries by observation – knowledge which, if properly used, could be more directly beneficial to mankind than all the other material sciences together, for it encompasses them all.

Worldwide literacy in astrology might well be a panacea for many of the unexplainable tensions which exist today between nations and individuals who claim to follow Him who cautioned man to "Love thy neighbor as thyself." Indeed historian Egon Freidell concludes that only through astrology can we find a solution to the present critical state of world civilization.[5]

The first scientific attempt to correlate the positions of the heavenly bodies with events on Earth was about 3300 BC when the Egyptians took the heliacal rising of Sirius, the Dog Star, as the beginning of their New Year. This event presaged the flooding of the Nile River, which was of major importance for Egyptian agriculture. Sirius is still thought to have a favorable influence on agriculture. Recognizable horoscopes have been found in Egypt dating from the Twelfth Dynasty, about 2500 BC, the most famous of which is in the Temple of Denderah (Figure 1).

In fragments of the document *Aegyptiaca*, attributed to the Egyptian priest Manetho,[6] there are claims that the Watchers or Angels came to Earth in the cosmic year 1000 (about 5500 BC) to converse with man and teach him about the luminaries and the zodiac signs.

While Indian astrology was once thought to be rooted in the astrology of Chaldea and Egypt, the researches of Alan Leo, Sepharial, and others show both systems to be original. Sepharial notes explicitly that Hindu astrology differs fundamentally from that handed down from Chaldea and Egypt,[7] although having identical meaning and yielding similar results when translated into the forms used by each school as well as by the occidental world today. Then, too, Sanskrit, the language of Hindu astrology, is in many respects the most highly developed language the world has known, while the "Chaldean and Hebrew tongues are in comparison as the lisping prattle of a child is to the mature diction of a philospher." Since language is the product of a people's thought this clearly indicates a native developmet of the science.

The *Pindayurdays*, dated 5500 BC, show Hindu astrology to have reached a high state of perfection at that time.

Figure 1. The circular zodiac found on the ceiling of the Temple of Denderah in Egypt. The North Pole is shown as having a hippopotamus in the center.

Chinese astrology developed independently, although there is evidence of early (2nd century BC) Greek influence through contacts with India.[8] Tradition assigns the formation of the constellations in China to Ta-jao, the prime minister of Hwang Ti (c 2637 BC), and makes much of an observation of the Pleiades in 2537 BC from an observatory said to have been erected in 2608 BC. However, proof of the independence of Chinese astronomy from Western influences is found in the names of the constellations. While the Sanskrit names for the signs of the zodiac are identical with their Greek counterparts the Chinese names are entirely different, being also based on a complete year rather than one month. The Chinese zodiac is the Dog, Cock Ape, Ram, Horse, Serpent, Dragon, Hare, Tiger, Ox, Rat, and Boar. They also use five elements rather than the four commonly considered in the West. The zodiac was known as the "Yellow Way", and progressed clockwise from the Rat.

The Japanese learned their astronomy and astrology from the Chinese. The earliest Japanese horoscope extant is dated 1112 AD, although references to the subject appear as early as 700 AD.

The Aztecs of the New World are known to have possessed an advanced calendar and it is speculated that they developed an astrology independent of the rest of the world. However, their writings were all destroyed by the Spaniards, so just how advanced their work was must remain a mystery.

Hebrew astrology, on the other hand, originated in Chaldea (Abraham was called from Ur of the Chaldees) and when the Jewish people broke the bonds of Egyptian serfdom they carried to the wilderness much of Egyptian methodology and philosophy. Notwithstanding admonitions against some Chaldean and other seers, soothsayers, and astrologers, scientific astrology was certainly practiced by the Jewish leaders. In the Book of Daniel we find that Daniel and his brethren in the Court of Nebuchadnezzar, ruler of Babylon, were *ten times* better astrologers than the best of the Babylonian magi or Chaldeans.[9] For further information about Hebrew astrology, the subject is treated very thoroughly by Sepharial.[10]

Greece borrowed its astrology from Egypt, as did the earlier Romans. The Greek philosophers did not at first look kindly upon astrology but gradually accepted it as the celestial science proved its value empirically. In consequence, Greek philosophy was modified along astrological lines and was thereby helped to reach the high position it held in later years.

In Egypt study of the stars had left an indelible imprint not only on astronomy but also on the development of higher mathematics. In Greece, the imprint was found in medicine and the herbal treatment of disease, in addition to philosophy. Hippocrates, generally considered the "Father of Medicine" and Pythagoras, one of the greatest mathematicians of all time, were among the greatest exponents of astrology. Aristotle referred to the circle of the zodiac. Euripides wrote that Hippo, daughter of Chiron, was able to prognosticate from the stars. According to Diodorus, the historian, (*circa* 30 BC), Chaldean astrologers foretold the death of Antigones, in 315 BC. Vitruvius recorded that astrology was brought to Greece by Berosus, a contemporary of Alexander the Great, who maintained a school of astrology on the island of Cos.

It was only natural for astrology to spread from Greece and Egypt to Italy and Rome. Cato, the Elder, mentioned it and Oneius Octavius was a follower of the science (as attested by the finding of a horoscope on his body after he was slain). Cicero referred to astrology, and Lucian stated that Julius Caesar observed the revolutions of the stars. Nigidius Figulus was one of the greatest astrologers of the later Roman Republic, foretelling the supremacy of Augustus Caesar. This same emperor also consulted the astrologer Theogenes, a citizen of Appolonia.

The greatest astrological work of all time was written by Claudius Ptolemy (c AD 150), a scholar in Alexandria which was then the world's center of learning. He was also a mathematician of great repute and brought to light the works of Hipparchus, who had lived some 200 years earlier. Ptolemy's most famous work, the *Almagest*, incorporated in a single volume the astrological knowledge known to the ancients, and from it later commentators have extracted the famous *Tetrabiblos*, or *Quadripartite: Four Books on the Influence of the Stars*. Since that time the *Tetrabiblos* of Ptolemy has been to astrology as the Bible is to Christianity. Every student should possess a copy of this famous book.[11]

Since the time of Ptolemy relatively little has been added to the basic science except as the result of additional planets (some of which were known as fixed stars by the ancients.)

While early man assumed the planetary energies to be Earth centered, or geocentric, rather than Sun centered, or heliocentric, they still recognized that their yearly seasons were related to the Vernal Equinox and this led Ptolemy to write, "It is reasonable to reckon the beginnings of the signs from the equinoxes and solstices, partly because the writers make this quite clear, and particularly, because from our previous demonstrations we observe that their natures, powers, and familiarities take their cause from the solstitial and equinoctial starting places, and from no other course. For if other starting places are assumed, we shall either be compelled no longer to use the natures of the signs for prognostications or, if we use them, to be in error."

Ennius, (239-169 BC) is the first Latin writer known to have mentioned astrology. Among those who spread astrology in Rome were slaves brought in from the East, and Pliny slates that the slave, Antiochos, was the one who introduced astrology to Italy. They were in trouble almost from the beginning; in 139 BC they were expelled from the city after being accused of fomenting a slave revolt. Both Augustus and Tiberius took measures against them, but the reason was to inhibit speculation concerning their death dates.

Thrasyllus was court astrologer to Tiberius, and the interesting tale of how he came to this post is told by Tacitus. Tiberius consulted several astrologers, decided that all were imposters, and had them quickly killed. Thrasyllus, in turn, predicted great glory for the Emperor. Thereupon Tiberius, to test him further, asked if Thrasyulls had cast his own nativity, and could he foresee what was going to happen to him in the course of that year? On that very day? Thrasyllus consulted his chart and "... striken with fear, he paused, hesitated, sank into meditation ... breaking his silence at last, he said, 'I see the crisis of my fate. This very moment may be my last' ... " Tiberius embraced him, congratulating him on his knowledge and his escape from danger. After that he regarded Thrasyllus' predictions as oracles of truth, and the astrologer was ranked high among his confidential friends.

Thrasyllus was a prolific writer on astrology. He accepted the views of the Egyptians, but in philosophy he was a neo-Pythagorean and even wrote a book on numerology. Porphyry (233-c. 304AD) cites him as an authority on Pythagoreanism and discusses the controversy waged by Ptolemy against the more occult aspects of the doctrines of Thrasyllus.

The first three centuries of the Christian era saw a systematic persecution in Rome of all astrologers who in any way became involved in imperial politics. Within the official circle, however, the astrologer became a powerful figure. Balbillus succeeded Thrasyllus as astrologer to Claudius and Nero. In fact, Nero's accession was planned by Agrippina with the aid of Balbillus and other astrologers, and the plot was postponed until the auspicious moment established by Balbillus. He was later instrumental in turning Nero against the Christians for allegedly starting the great fire of AD 64. This, of course, did not endear astrology to the Christians.

Despite the efforts of Porphyry (in his *Tetrabiblos of Ptolemy*) to introduce science into Roman astrology, the latter in this period combined Stoic fatalism with Egyptian superstition. These trends reached a culmination in the reign of Caracalla (AD 188-217) who ascended the throne through the murder of his brother, Geta, in AD 212. During his reign astrology came under the influence of various cults devoted to the worship of the Moon, the Sun, and Heracles. Although the art had a powerful grip on the Romans, it degenerated into necromancy, magic chants, and other superstitions.

Astrology again came into conflict with Christianity in the end of the third century with the advent of the neo–Gnostic sect known as Manichaeism. Gnosticism was a religious movement older than Christianity, combining elements from a number of other doctrines. In some Gnostic sects only the elect who have been initiated into the mysteries can be saved, and this elect band usually operated through secret magic rites and formulae. When Christianity appeared, it is speculated that the Gnostics adapted their philosophy to the new religion, appealing to those who wished to consider themselves superior to their fellow beings. The Persian, Mani (c. AD 250), attempted to fuse the teachings of Zoroaster with those of Christ. From the Christian point of view his heresies were many, but here we need only note that astology played a prominent part in the secret Manichaean rituals. Astrology then, according to Mani, was not a science open to all but secret knowledge accessible only to a select few.

Constantine the Great legalized Christianity in 313 AD by the Edict of Milan, and in 325 he convoked the epoch-making Council of Nicea which formalized Christian doctrine in the Nicean Creed and condemned the heresies of Gnosticism and Manichaeism. By implication astrology was also condemned, but this was the astrology practised by the superstitious or heretical cults and not the astrology of Ptolemy. Thus it was an astrology with occasional validity but whose philosophical basis was anathema to science. The Catholic church has always, and will always condemn superstition, and astrology has often been espoused by charlatans who associated themselves with pseudoscience and occultism in order to line their pockets. Consequently, it has often been mistaken for that with which it was associated.

The Roman Empire did not disappear at once but slowly sank into oblivion. Its great artists and poets were no more, and the many centuries of moral decay left the once great city bereft of its inheritance from earlier times. Christianity became the state religion, but the Holy Fathers were interested in man's relationship with God more than in his relationship with the world. The monasteries kept knowledge alive but did nothing to advance the level of scholarship in any field other than theology. As is so often the case when church and state are fused, heresy was considered akin to treason. Gnosticism and Manichaeism were suppressed and, with them, knowledge of their system of astrology. That many in the church were concerned by the revival of pseudo-astrology with its attendant heresy is attested by the fact that in England the Venerable Bede (673-135) attempted to substitute the names of the apostles for the signs of the zodiac: Peter (Aries), Andrew (Taurus), James the Greater (Gemini), John (Cancer), Thomas (Leo) James the Lesser (Virgo), Philip (Libra), Bartholomew (Scorpio), Matthew (Sagittarius), Simon (Capricorn), John the Baptist as a substitute for Judas (Aquarius), and Jude (Pisces).

The pre-Islamic Arabs, however, were very familiar with Greek science, particularly with Ptolemy and Aristotle. The neo–Platonic philosopher, Stephanus of Alexandria, who was a contemporary of Heraclius (610)-(641), in the fall of 621 calculated a horoscope for the birth of Islam. From this chart, cast six months prior to the Hegira, Stephanus correctly predicted the course of Islam through the Abbasid Caliphate in 755. Included in his predictions were the battles of Jalula (637), Nahavend (641), and the civil war of 660; also the defeat of Suleiman at the gates of Constantinople (717-718) and the preservation of Christianity through the defeat of Abd al–Rahman by Charles Martel at Tours in 732.

Astrology was well established as a scientific discipline in Islam during the European Dark Ages. Al–Kindi (d. 873) was a great Arabic follower of Aristotle. Of the tribe of Kindah, he wrote on geometry, astronomy, arithmetic, music (which he developed on mathematical principles), physics, medicine, psychology, meteorology, and politics. Although this is not discussed in scientific circles today, al–Kindi also wrote several treatises on astrology, summarizing this knowledge in the light of current science.

But perhaps the greatest Arabic astrologer was a follower of al–Kindi, Muhammed ibn Ahmad al–Biruni. Al–Biruni traveled to India and wrote a commentary on Indian science and astrology. Of more interest to us is his great work on astrology: *The Book of Instruction in the Elements of the Art of Astrology*, written in 1029 but translated into English only in 1934 (by R. Ramsay Wright). Not more than one hundred copies of the English translation are extant. This work contains many elements of astrology not to be found in the more modern books, and some of the astrological techniques in use today differ greatly from those of al–Biruni. A complete discussion of these matters would take us far afield. Al–Biruni, in any case, was a true student of Ptolemy and fully recognized the place of astrology in the scheme of scientific knowledge. His book is in five parts: mathematics, astronomy, geography, chronology, and astrology, and this is not accidental, since, following Ptolemy, al–Biruni viewed astrology not as a science in itself but rather as an extension of other scientific disciplines.

With the rise of Islam, Israel left the yoke of Rome to be taken into the camp of the Prophet, bringing along Jewish expertise in philosophy, science, and astrology. The most famous Jewish astrologer of the Middle Ages was Masha'allah (known to Europe as Messahala) who wrote an astrological world history with the title: *On Conjunctions, Religions, and Peoples*. Showing that all important religious and political changes are indicated by the conjunctions of Saturn and Jupiter, this work related the history of the world from the Deluge (c. 3380 BC) to the rise of the Buwayhids (AD 928). Masha'allah also completed accession horoscopes for the caliphs through Harun al–Rashid and wrote a book on nativities.

Through the Jewish astrologers Europe again learned of the scientific astrology of Ptolemy. Of these the most influential was the poet, mathematician, and philosopher, Abraham ben Meir ibn Ezra (1092-1167) whose philosophical influence was restricted to the Jewish world. To the Christians he was known mainly as an astrologer. He made significant contributions to exegesis, philosophy, philology, grammar, poetry, and mathematics. He was one of the most famous Jews of any time or any clime, and the great orientalist, Leopold Dukes, has written of him:

"Every literature occasionally has a man to boast of, who equipped with the knowledge of his time, finds himself in a position to survey it, although his age is unable to appreciate him. Such men see far beyond the intellectual horizon of their contemporaries and hang aloft their lantern, from which later generations kindle their light. Such a man was Abraham ibn Ezra."[12]

Ibn Ezra was inclined toward judicial astrology but also wrote on nativities. He wrote eight astrological treatises in Hebrew: *The Beginning of Wisdom, The Book of Reasons, The Book of Nativities, The Book of Consultations of the Stars, The Book of Selections, The Book of Lights, The Book of the World,* and *The Conjunctions.*

His astrology is basically that of Ptolemy, with the latter's pure rationalism being significantly modified by large doses of Jewish mysticism and a tendency to Stoic fatalism –elements present even today in most books on astrology. This mysticism does not go as far as the occultism of the Egyptians, nor is the fatalism as absolute as that of the Stoics and Gnostics. Indeed, the sophisticated Hebrew scholar would not regard these as superstitions at all. But Renaissance man was not sophisticated, and his interpretation of ibn Ezra yielded an astrology marked by just these qualities –which necessarily came into conflict with the mechanistic materialism of the eighteenth and nineteenth centuries.

The treatises of ibn Ezra were translated into French in 1273. Of these, *The Beginning of Wisdom* contains 120 aphorisms useful in prognostics which were later taken up by Johannes Campanus (c. 1260) who testified of their reliability to Pope Urban IV. This Pope made Campanus his personal physician and philosopher. Campanus was also a mathematician noted for his translation of Euclid. In astrology he invented a method of house division based on trisection of the prime vertical. As Ptolemy's method of house division had not yet been distributed in Europe, Campanus had to improvise on the basis of the incomplete descriptions in ibn Ezra. But he was successful and thereby promoted a revival of scientific astrology in Western Europe.

While Pope Leo X was still a small child, the astrologer Marsilio Ficino predicted to his father, Lorenzo the Magnificent, that the little Giovanni would one day wear the papal tiara. The date of Julius II's coronation was astrologically selected. Alexander IV kept Cardinal Bianco in the Vatican for astrological prognostications, while Sixtus IV chose the proper planetary times for all his audiences, and Paul III did the same for every papal consistory.

Pope Calixtus III ordered prayers and anathemas against astrological predictions of Turkish success over the Knights Templars. Cardinal d'Ailly calculated a horoscope for Jesus Christ.

Every scientist was first an astrologer. Every astronomer prior to, and including, Kepler was an astrologer. Tycho Brahe (1546-1601), one of the greatest Renaissance astronomers, wrote: "To doubt the influence of the stars is to doubt the wisdom and providence of God." Brahe was an extraordinary observer of the heavens and invented various non-telescopic instruments that allowed him to determine the positions in the sky of celestial bodies with an average error of less than a minute of arc. These observations led him also to discard the Ptolemaic system but, rather than repudiate the geocentric system completely (with Copernicus), Brahe made the planets revolve around the sun while the latter in turn revolved around a stationary earth. He made most of his observations from the island of Hven northeast of Copenhagen. Brahe was also an excellent astrologer, having predicted accurately the achievements and time of death of Gustavus Adolphus, and was invited to the court of Rudolf II of Austria.

Brahe brought with him as protege a young astronomer who was already being talked about for his brilliant theories: Johann Kepler (1571-1630). While Brahe took on Kepler because of his abilities as an astronomer, the Emperor Rudolf agreed to the appointment because of his competence as an astrologer. Kepler had already prophesied from the stars a hard winter, and so it proved. He had also prepared horoscopes for the great Wallenstein and other German notables. Therefore, it is not surprising that Kepler's first assignment was in astrology: in 1602 he published his *De fundamentis astrologiae certioribus* whose aim was "to distill and preserve" the truths of astrology. In 1603 Kepler wrote the *Judicium de trigonoigneo* proposing what are today called the minor aspects: semi-quartile (semi–square), sesquiquadrate, quincunx, and semi-sextile.

Two years after Kepler's arrival in Prague Brahe died and left the records of his life's work to his protege. Using the detailed observations of his master, especially those on Mars, Kepler was able to formulate his first two laws of planetary motion. Published in 1600 in *Astronomia nova*, these are:

(1) The orbit of each planet is an ellipse with the Sun at one of its foci.

(2) Each planet revolves so that the line joining it to the Sun sweeps over equal areas in equal intervals of time.

Further study enabled Kepler to publish, in 1619 (*De Hannonice mundi*), his third law from which Newton was later to develop the law of gravitation:

(3) The squares of the periods of any two planets are in the same proportions as the cubes of their mean distances from the Sun.

Kepler's first love was astronomy, although he continued to publish treatises in astrology (i.e., *Tertius interveniens*, 1610). Both sciences claim Kepler as one of their own - and both are correct!

But this story would not be complete without a reference to Galileo Galilei (1564- 1642) who invented the telescope and whose observations of the phases of Venus completely discredited Ptolemaic astronomy. Centuries earlier, Saint Augustine and Thomas Aquinas had written that the Bible was not supposed to be used to teach science, and its authority should not be invoked in scientific disputes. But neither Galileo nor the Church were willing to heed these admonitions. What could not be demonstrated by scientific observation could be proven by holy scripture, and Galileo took up the cause of Copernicus with fervent zeal. But he was no match here for his enemies within the Church, and even his friend, Pope Urban VIII, was forced to give in. He was censured for his views and prohibited from promulgating them in any form.

Thus Copernicus introduced the hypothesis of a heliocentric universe, Kepler developed the theory from the observations of Brahe, and Galileo's new invention of the telescope provided the experimental evidence. The science of astronomy, as well as all human knowledge, was on the verge of a revolution.

Astrology, nonetheless, continued to flourish. Jean Baptiste Morin de Villefranche (1583-1656), the author of *Astrologia Gallica*, correctly predicted the deaths of Richelieu, Louis XIII, and Wallenstein. Another authority was the monk, Placidus de Tito (l603–1668), a professor of mathematics at the University of Padua. Both invented systems of house division which still bear their names, although that of Placidus is the better known today.

Perhaps the most historically significant blow against scientific astrology was that dealt by Sir Isaac Newton (1642-1727) who, together with Leibnitz in Germany, developed the mathematics of the infinitesimal, today called calculus. He applied this tool to the observations of Kepler and Galileo to formulate the laws of motion and gravitation in his great work, *Philosophiae naturalis principia mathematica*.

Newton himself never intended this consequence, as he himself was deeply interested in astrology and wrote many treatises on the subject (which have not yet been published). But the new theories used calculus to achieve a rigor in the physical sciences that had never before been possible. The real intellectual challenge was seen to be the development of mathematics and physics based on Newtonian mechanics, and scientists since that day have largely abandoned the serious study of astrology. Those who still regarded as valid the correlations of the heavenly bodies with events on earth had no time to apply themselves to astrology, and it was left to those with little or no scientific training.

Roger Bacon, who lived in the thirteenth century, was an astrologer. The Franciscan monk, Guido Bonatus, prognosticated by astrology in about 1300 AD and left us works on the subject.[13] Valuable astrological works were left by Henry Cornelius Agrippa who was also a famous occult philosopher, living from 1486 to 1535. He was court astrologer to Francis I of France but was dismissed for his correct forecasts of events unfavorable to that ruler. Florent de Villiers was another known French astrologer at the court of Louis XI.

The best known French astrologer was Nostradamus (Michel de Nostredame), physician to Henry II, who reached the pinnacle of his fame about 1555. Queen Catherine de Medici made him her special favorite. He was the greatest of the "long distance" prognosticators, his prophecies being written in a thousand four line stanzas entitled *Seven Centuries of Prophecies*.[14] Included were prophecies of the execution of Charles I of England, one hundred years before it occurred, and of the exact date of the founding of the French Republic, more than two hundred years before it occurred. But most remarkable of all, from the American standpoint, was his prognostication of our Civil War, its length, and its devastation. He wrote: "About that time (1861) a great quarrel and contest will arise in a country beyond the seas (America). Many poor devils will be hung and many poor wretches killed by a punishment other than the cord.

Upon my faith you may believe me, the war will not cease for four years at which none should be astonished or surprised, for there will be no want of hatred or obstinacy in it. At the end of that time, prostrate and almost ruined, the people will embrace each other in great joy and love." An analysis of the works of Nostradamus suggests that he was familiar with the works of Masha'sllah.

Goethe began his autobiography"[15] with the statement: "On the 28th of August, 1749, at mid-day, as the clock struck twelve, I came into the world, at Frankfort–am-Main. The aspect of the stars was propitious; the Sun stood in the sign of the Virgin, and had culminated for the day; Jupiter and Venus looked on him with a friendly eye, and Mercury not adversely; the attitude of Saturn and Mars was neutral; the Moon alone, just full, exerted all the more her power of opposition as she had just reached her planetary hour. She, therefore, resisted my birth which could not be accomplished until this hour was passed. These auspicious aspects which the astrologers subsequently interpreted very favorably for me may have been the causes of my preservation."

In England Lord Burleigh calculated the horoscopes of Queen Elizabeth and other royalty. Mr. John Dee, who was in many ways a charlatan and one of those responsible for bringing the science into disrepute, lived during this period, dying in 1608. Elias Ashmole of Oxford refers to the annual Astrologers' Feast, mentioning the Reverend M. Butler, Sir Edmund Deering, and many other eminent people of the day.

William Lilly, born in 1602, whose works are still consulted,[16] was the greatest of the early English astrologers. Charles I consulted Lilly in 1647 and 1648 concerning his own safety but ignored the advice (after promising to follow it) and was beheaded. Lilly writes that "for very great considerations the Council of State gave me (in 1648) in money fifty pounds, and a pension of one hundred pounds per annum, which for two years I received, but no more." In 1651 Lilly predicted the black plague and the Great Fire of London which occurred only in 1665-1666. After the fire Lilly was summoned before the House of Commons committee investigating it; the Committee Chairman, Sir Robert Brooke, stating: 'You are called the rather hinter, because, in a book of yours long since printed you hinted some such thing."

Many other famous names, such as Galileo, Bacon, Newton, Copernicus, and Flammarion, are associated with astrology. Flamsted, the first Astronomer Royal of England, selected on astrological grounds the date for building the Greenwich Observatory, and that original horoscope written in his own hand is now a cherished possession of the British Museum. The wisdom of his choice is seen in the fact that Greenwich today is the point from which virtually all astronomical calculations are based throughout the world.

Astrology was undoubtedly a greater factor in the Reformation than historians have been willing to acknowledge.

During the nineteenth century astrological calculation was simplified, and the science popularized for the masses, through the research and study of more than a score of English astrologers – notably, Raphael (R. C. Smith), Zadkiel (Morrison), Sepharial (Green), and others.

There is little awareness of astrology's imprint upon modern civilization. The calendar used today throughout the Christian world, and the feasts of the Christian church, have their origin in astrology. This celestial science has been scorned, scoffed at, and even persecuted in every age, yet it thrives today among people of learning and profound intellectual capacity to a far greater extent than is commonly realized. A 1927 census of persons in the United States actively interested in the science revealed a figure of 443,000, and this total has undoubtedly increased many times since.

The nature of astrology has enabled it to become a weapon in the hands of charlatans. This has brought upon the science the same kind of criticism as may be found in the Old Testament; but it is now definitely proven that Judaism used astrology – even in connection with its most sacred rituals. The original Jewish criticism of false prophets of astrology continued into medieval times when the pervasive ignorance only accentuated the influence of those believed to possess occult and supernatural powers. Although the science was used openly by scientists and high Church and State officials, it was forbidden to the masses (although no Papal edict was ever issued against it) because of the ease with which imposters could pervert it for their own purposes. In the fourteenth century some astrologers were tortured and even burned at the stake, this persecution reaching its height under the Inquisition when exponents of the science *outside* the ecclesiastical establishment were boiled in oil or broken on the wheel while those *inside* it were being steadily consulted.

At this very day the uneducated, superstitious, and fearful stand in awe at the apparently miraculous abilities of the scientific student of this subject. But criticism is justified of the many who claim a profound knowledge of the science and yet misread or misrepresent the meaning of horoscopes and pervert astrology for their own aggrandizement.

Notwithstanding the assaults – almost always by the uninformed or misinformed – the ancient science of astrology has developed steadily.[17] Interest in it has intensified due to the stimulus of the early nineteenth century leaders and the archaeological research done in the last fifty years. In the Aquarian Age (Aquarius rules the air, electricity, invention, and the higher planes of artistic production, as well as astrology itself) it will once again assume its rightful place as a valuable aid to civilization, and it may well be this age's guide out of the crass materialism into which it is plunged.

The sole aim of this book is to stimulate interest in astrology and simplify its study, learn to erect horoscopes, and trace the planetary influences on personal lives. Every man and woman should have at least a working knowledge of the subject. It should be taught in every high school in the land. Experimentation with one's own chart for the period already lived will show the trend of influences which the future will bring to bear. Such knowledge is like a weather map indicating the air currents and cross–currents which the pilot must face in order to guide the airplane to its destination. One word of caution seems advisable: *The true astrologer does not tell the future*, he simply indicates influences. The author of this book has no sympathy with so-called fortune telling. This was well stated by A.G. Trent, Secretary to the British Museum, in his Preface to Wilde's volume on *Chaldean Astrology*:

'Nothing – has brought scientific astrology into such disrepute as the notion that it is an occult science. It is nothing of the kind. An occult science is one that can be pursued only by adepts. Astrology is just as much a physical science as astronomy or geology. It depends, like them, upon the evidence of ascertained facts, and has so far the advantage of its sister sciences that those facts are patent to the observation of everybody, and that its rules and methods can be mastered by any person of average intelligence."

Astrology explains the universe; the little understood laws of the Creator. It explains the marvelous teachings of the Man of Nazareth, and it explains the harmony of good. It is not a religion, and yet it encompasses the fundamentals of all religions. Man is the master of his own destiny, and "the stars only impel, but do not compel." Drifters follow unresistingly the malefic influences as well as the benefic. Astrology indicates the influences and points out how to overcome the malefic while turning the benefic to use. It teaches us that so–called malefic influences are only maladjusted cosmic forces which can be overcome.

The wise man rules his stars, the fool permits his stars to rule him.

Review Questions for Chapter 1

1. Why is astrology sometimes called a pseudo-science?

2. Is the practice of astrology against the tenets of traditional Christianity? Explain.

3. How did Newton's discoveries change the emphasis of scientific thinking?

4. Trace the thread of philosophical thought as it turned to astrology during the Grecian age to the modern trend.

5. Who are some of the men prominent in the study of astrology through the ages?

Chapter 2

Houses of the Horoscope

Two systems of astrology are used in the West: **Geocentric** and **Heliocentric**. As these words imply, geocentric means centered on Earth and deals with the *apparent* motion of all celestial bodies around Earth. Heliocentric means centered on the Sun and deals with the *actual* motion of all the bodies of the solar system around the Sun.

The geocentric system (Figure 2) is the one in general use, and it offers two methods for erecting a horoscope: the **Fixed Ascendant** chart and the **Fixed Sign** chart. The former is used throughout the occidental world, but the latter has some advantages for research involving the comparison of horoscopes. This text employs the simple fixed Ascendant method; with the aid of the modern astrological ephemerides and the rules included in this course of instruction almost anyone can learn to erect an accurate horoscope.

Although the Sun is the center of the solar system, (as seen in Figure 3), every day the Sun, Moon, planets, and stars appear to make one complete revolution around the earth from east to west. This is, of course, due to the earth's rotation on its axis from west to east. The relations among the planets, and between the planets and the point on the earth's surface for which the horoscope is calculated, will be the same in both the geocentric and the heliocentric systems. Therefore, on the theory that astrology is concerned with the action of the planets upon the earth considered as a passive recipient, the system taught in the following pages will be based on the geocentric positions of the planets. [18]

Before the student proceeds further, however, his attention should be directed to the interrelations among the four sciences, including astrology, concerned with the study of the heavenly phenomena. Dr. Francis Rolt–Wheeler, formerly of the *Institut Astrologique de Carthage*, has described these four sciences as follows and grateful acknowledgment is made here of his kind permission to quote the following passages:

Astronomy deals with the real and apparent movements of the heavenly bodies; the laws which govern them; their sizes, masses, volumes and densities; their natures and physical conditions; their interrelations and mutual effects; together with the heavenly phenomena such as occultations, eclipses, etc. It deals, moreover, with the application of those astronomical conditions to earthly conditions, especially in geodesy and navigation.

Astrology deals with the relations between these heavenly bodies and all living creatures and terrestrial objects, but especially man. It treats particularly of the complex rhythms of the universe as they influence man in his physical, mental, and spiritual capacities and, since these rhythms are constant and can be calculated in advance, it considers equally the past, the present, and the future.

Astrognosy treats principally of the symbolism of astrology and of the occult teaching hidden under this symbolism; it endeavors to penetrate the meanings which form the laws of astronomy and astrology.

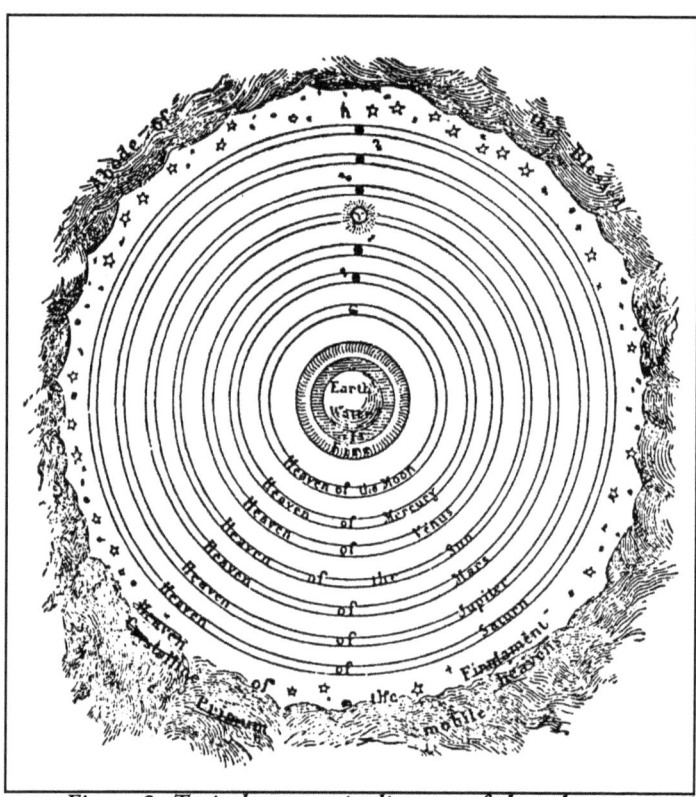

Figure 2. Typical geocentric diagram of the solar system. A nineteenth century depiction of the Ptolemaic conception of the universe with Earth at the center.

Astrosophy is the philosophical branch of this group of studies. It uses the calculations and the findings of astronomy, the science and the art of astrology, and the secrets of astrognosy with the purpose of extending the horizon of human thought and of rendering more comprehensible the fundamental reason for human existence and thus illuminating the truths of life.

This course, however, deals only with astrology. The science and art of astrology may be further divided into special branches, each complete in itself and in each of which the horoscope is methodically the same:

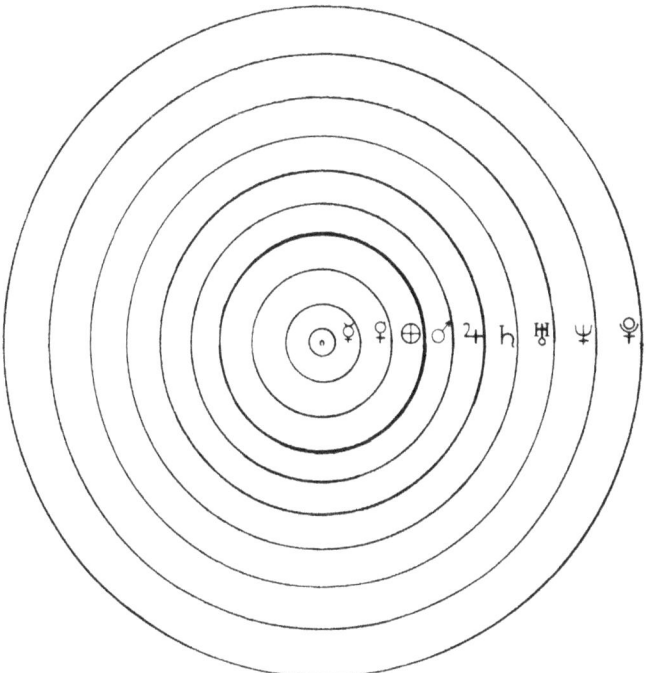

Figure 3. A heliocentric diagram of the solar system showing the Sun in the center surrounded by the planets.

Genethliacal or Natal Astrology is based upon a celestial map drawn for the individual's moment, date, and place of birth. It deals with the person's physical characteristics, mental qualities, and spiritual development as well as indicating the nature of the influences affecting his life.

Pre-Natal Astrology is based upon a celestial map drawn for the moment of astrological conception, this being calculated from a natal horoscope. It deals almost exclusively with the individuality, the soul, or the inner character of the native.

Horary Astrology is based upon a celestial map drawn for the moment when a question of importance or concern is submitted or the moment of an event, on the theory that planetary influences cause the matter to be discussed or to occur and that the positions of the celestial bodies at this time indicate the influences affecting the outcome of this event or the persons connected with it.

Political or Mundane Astrology is based upon a celestial map drawn for the moment, date, and place of founding of a community, nation, organization, or other group, and deals with the influences affecting the life of such a group. This system uses other cyclic maps, such as the moment of the Vernal Equinox, lunations, full moons, eclipses, etc, and they are always calculated for the meridian of the seat of government or for the geographical coordinates of the location.

Medical Astrology is a specialized branch of natal astrology based upon the natal horoscope but dealing entirely with the prevention and healing of the individual's physical, mental, or emotional ailments. Indeed, astrology is the mother of medicine as early herbal practice arose out of astrology. Unbeknownst to most students, the present-day foundation of biochemistry is laid over an astrological basis. Since this branch of the science is more than mere medicine, the author terms it Pathological Astrology.

Astro–Meteorology is that branch of the science which deals with prediction of the weather and of such terrestrial phenomena as earthquakes, floods, fires, etc, over which man has little or no control.

Having completed these explanations, let us now consider the factors entering into a horoscope. The student should bear firmly in mind that a horoscope is only a celestial map – usually of just the solar system along the ecliptic, with the addition of certain other sensitive points – for the subject's moment and place of birth.

Maps of the earth place the east on the right, the west on the left, the north at the top, and the south at the bottom. But since celestial maps represent the "inverted bowl of heaven," they always place the east (*horizon*) on the left, the west (*horizon*) on the right, the **Zenith** at the top, and the **Nadir** at the bottom. The subject's place of birth is at the center of the map, and the eastern horizon (left) is called the **Ascendant**. The western horizon (right), its complement or opposite point, is the **Descendant**. The **Medium Coeli (MC)** or **Midheaven**, is the highest point of the heavens on precisely the meridian for which the chart is calculated. It is the Sun's location at noon and its complement, the **Imum Coeli (IC)** or **Nadir**, is the exact opposite, the Sun's location at midnight.

The Midheaven is also known as the **South** point of the chart, since above 23° N 27' the degree of the ecliptic at that point is always due south of the place for which the chart is calculated. Similarly, the Nadir is known as the **North** point. This is illustrated graphically by Figure 4.

It will be noted that the horoscope circle is thus divided into four equal divisions, each 90 degrees in extent, known as the **Four Quadrants**. Also, a cross is formed within the circle which is known as the Horoscope Cross.

Each quadrant is further divided into three equal parts, and these twelve mundane divisions in the completed chart are known as the twelve **Houses** or **Mansions** (sometimes confus-

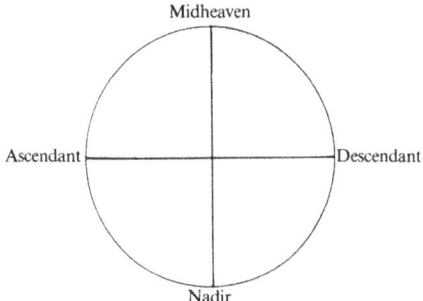

Figure 4. Celestial map of the four quadrants, showing the Midheaven, Ascendant, Descendant, and Nadir in their proper positions. The Horoscope Cross.

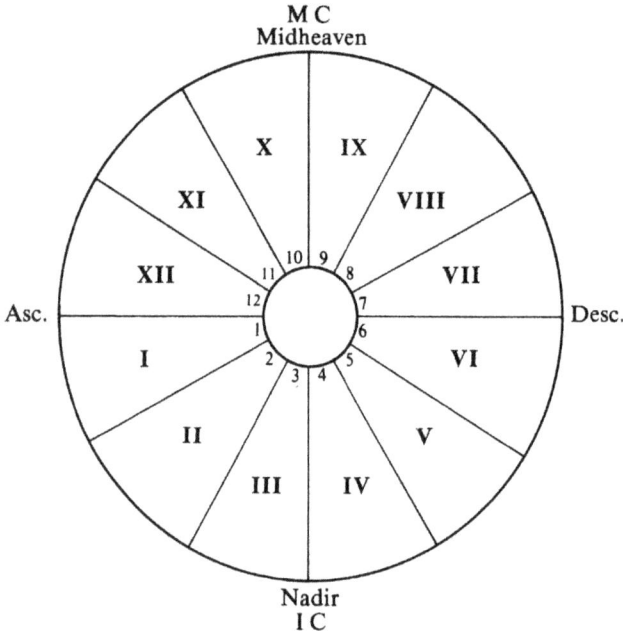

Figure 5. The twelve houses of the horoscope.

ingly termed "quarters"). These twelve houses are fixed with each covering 30 degrees of the horoscope circle measured in oblique ascension. This is illustrated by Figure 5.

The houses are seen to be numbered (preferably in Roman numerals to avoid later confusion with other numbers) counter-clockwise starting with the Ascendant.

The earth rotates once on its axis in each period of approximately 24 hours, and a person at a given point on the earth's surface would see the complete canopy of the heavens pass by during that time. The Sun, the Moon, each of the planets, and the entire host of stars, as well as the twelve divisions of the zodiac in which the planets and luminaries are measured, would come to the eastern horizon, appear to ascend to the Midheaven (MC), descend to the western horizon, pass under the earth to the Nadir (IC), and then reappear on the eastern horizon. Each day, therefore, all the celestial bodies and the twelve signs of the zodiac appear to pass through the twelve houses of the horoscope chart.

Referring to Figure 5, the student will note that houses, I, IV, VII, and X start at the divisions (known as **cusps**) which make up the four arms of the Horoscope Cross (as in Figure 4). These houses, known as **ANGULAR**, strengthen the influence of the planets and signs found in them.

Houses II, V, VIII, and XI, known as **SUCCEDENT**, are less strong; while houses III, VI, IX, and XII, called **CADENT**, are weakest in influence.

The order of houses in strength is thus: I, X, VII, IV, XI, VIII, II, V, III, IX, VI and XII. There has always been some difference of opinion as to the relative strength of houses I and X, Ptolemy pointing out that a planet in the tenth is stronger than one in the first or Ascendant. This, however, will necessarily depend upon the nature of the chart as a whole (see also below, comments on house I).

House strength, however, is subsidiary to the sign strength of planets. A planet strong by sign position and weak by house position is always stronger than one which is weak by sign position and strong by house position, other factors being equal, and unless the planets are in angular houses and strongly aspected.

The student must also remember that under the fixed Ascendant method of erecting a horoscope the houses are always constant. They do not shift position with the planets and stars, and each covers precisely 30 degrees of the horoscope circle measured in oblique ascension.

The houses of the horoscope relate particularly to the **material** and **physical** conditions of life, while the zodiacal signs are primarily related to the higher qualities as manifested in **character**. The houses also indicate the avenues of life through which various influences will be manifested.

It will also be noted that each quadrant (one fourth) of the horoscope contains three houses: one angular, one succedent, and one cadent. Furthermore, each quadrant has particular significance in itself (used primarily in connection with the very limited number of charts encountered in which very many planets are grouped in a single quadrant) and, although rarely used, they indicate life emphasis as follows:

The lower-east (Northeast) quadrant is personal (houses I, II, III)

The lower-west (Northwest) quadrant is companionate (houses IV, V, VI)

The upper-west (Southwest) quadrant is companionate-personal (houses VII, VIII, IX)

The upper-east (Southeast) quadrant is personal-companionate (houses X, XI, XII)

The meaning of these indications will become clear as the individual houses are studied carefully. The two upper quadrants, above the horizon, are termed "above the earth" and the planets and zodiacal signs found in them indicate prominence – the public side of life. The two lower quadrants, below the horizon, are termed "below the earth" and tend to indicate the obscure phases of life – private life or retirement.

The house divisions and influences are as follows:

HOUSE I

The FIRST HOUSE is generally known as the Ascendant. It rules the early life and childhood of the individual, particularly the first seven years. Together with the fourth house, it has dominion over environment during these first years and thus largely controls the development of personality and disposition. It rules the physical body and constitution generally, and the head in particular, but to a lesser extent than the first zodiacal sign Aries. It is the house of health, as distinguished from the sixth house, which is the house of ill health.

The first, fourth, seventh, and tenth houses are the strongest in the horoscope, since through them life finds its fullest expression in: (I) personality, (IV) home, (VII) marriage and relationship to others, and (X) profession, honor, and attainment. But this does not mean that these houses are more important per se than the others, for the twelve are a whole, and to consider any one of them less important than the others would weaken or destroy that portion of the delineation.

As the first house is on the eastern arm of the Horoscope Cross, the angular position tends to strengthen planets found therein.

HOUSE II

The SECOND HOUSE rules the native's finances in the sense of wealth earned by his own efforts. It indicates the prospects for acquiring and holding money or possessions of value and, in this sense, expresses the liberty of the individual. The desire for wealth is also expressed through this house. It is a house of material interests.

The second house is the natural home of the second zodiacal sign, Taurus, and thus has much in common with the attributes of Taurus, particularly rulership over the throat, upper bronchii, and the base of the brain. It is also called the *nocturnal house* of Venus.

Since the second house is succedent, planets found in it are less strong by house position than those found in angular houses.

HOUSE III

The THIRD HOUSE is more varied in its rulership, having to do with brothers, sisters, relatives generally (except parents), neighbors, travel (especially short journeys over land), letters, papers, publications, literature, writing, and other matters of the concrete mind. It is best known for its relationship to mental attributes and is thus called the **House of Concrete Mind**.

Its harmony with the third zodiacal sign, Gemini, gives it influence over teaching and mental ability generally. It is also called the *diurnal house* of Mercury.

This house also rules matters relating to mail-order enterprises, transportation, railways, automobiles, and all means of communication. Physically, it rules the lungs, nerves, arms, and shoulders. As it is cadent, planets found in the third house are weakest by house position.

HOUSE IV

The FOURTH HOUSE rules the place and circumstances of birth and death as well as the environment and home of the native, particularly toward the close of life. It also rules the parent of the opposite sex, unless the zodiacal sign Cancer is on the cusp, in which case it rules the mother. Some competent astrologers, including the late Alan Leo, consider the fourth house to rule the mother in all charts. This is not borne out by the author's experience, however, since the Sun (ruler of Leo) and the Moon (ruler of Cancer) are often definite indicators of the father and mother (respectively) regardless of the sign on the cusp of the fourth house. Saturn has also been found to be the indicator of one of the parents, particularly the father, probably because it not only represents older people but is also the natural ruler of the tenth house.

The fourth house is sometimes called "the grave" because of its relationship to the hidden or private side of life and death, the end of all things. It is also associated with ownership of land, property, and mines.

Being the natural home of Cancer, the fourth sign of the zodiac, the fourth house has some of the attributes of that sign. It is often called the *natural house* of the Moon. Physically, it rules the chest, breasts, stomach, and liver.

HOUSE V

The FIFTH HOUSE rules the native's offspring, courtship, and love affairs outside wedlock. It rules women generally (especially in a male chart), the physical and emotional pleasures, theaters and other places of amusement, luxuries of various kinds, schools and education, speculation, gambling, and investments.

Relationship with the zodiacal sign Leo gives it many of the Leo attributes.

It is also called the *natural house* of the Sun. The fifth house is succedent, and the planets found there are less strong than those found in angular houses. Physically, the fifth house rules the heart and the back.

HOUSE VI

The SIXTH HOUSE is called an unfortunate house, as it rules the native's ill health, (the health we have as a result of our own doing). Since it may produce handicaps which are difficult to overcome, it influences the strength of houses I and X.

While the fifth house rules eating, drinking, and clothing as pleasures, the sixth house rules them as necessities. In fact, it rules all necessities. This is the **House of Service**, in respect of the native himself and of his relations with employees and servants. It is the house of labor and of debt, as well as of small and domestic animals.

The foregoing indicates how easily this house can cause worry and petty annoyances, particularly when afflicted.

The sixth house has much in common with the sixth zodiacal sign, Virgo, and thus takes on many of the latter's attributes. It is also called the *nocturnal house* of Mercury. Physically, it rules the bowels and solar plexus.

HOUSE VII

The SEVENTH HOUSE is generally termed the **House of Marriage** because it rules contracts, partnerships, and agreements of all kinds. It rules the marriage partner as well as local and state laws concerned with marital rights and responsibilities. The house of individuality, it also rules the public and the native's relationship to the public. It indicates open enemies, rivals, and competitors, as well as thieves, robbers, and litigation.

The seventh house is on the western arm of the Horoscope Cross and is consequently angular, strengthening the planets found in it.

It takes on some of the attributes of the zodiacal sign, Libra, and physically has rulership over the bladder, kidneys, and vital fluids of the body. It is also called the *diurnal house* of Venus.

As the first house represents "self," so the seventh house represents "others," the complement of self or "other self."

HOUSE VIII

The EIGHTH HOUSE is the second of the so-called unfortunate houses, as it rules death, dissolution, and losses, as well as legacies, bequests, wills, and the property of the dead. Its connection with the physical death of the native associates it with latent occult ability and regeneration. Here, however, it must be remembered that, as the Ascendant is the **Point of life**, so its complement, the Descendant or seventh house cusp, is the **Point of Death**.

Just as the seventh house rules the marriage partner, so the eighth house rules the marriage partner's second house affairs (wealth and finance) and thus indicates dowry in those countries where this custom still exists.

With the zodiacal sign, Scorpio, being the natural ruler of the eighth house, it takes on some of the Scorpio attributes. It is the natural house of Pluto, and the ancients called it the *nocturnal house* of Mars. This house is succedent and planets found therein are less strong by house position. Physically it is associated with matters of sex and the procreative organs.

HOUSE IX

Just as the third house rules the concrete mind so its complement, the NINTH HOUSE, rules the abstract mind, the higher self, true religion, and philosophy. It governs idealism, philanthropy, dreams, visions, psychic experiences, higher education, personal cultivation and development, and the fine arts, thus controlling the philosophic, philanthropic, and spiritual tendencies of the native. The clergy and church matters are here indicated.

While the third house rules short journeys, particularly by land, the ninth governs journeys far from the birthplace, particularly by sea, as well as travel in foreign countries. It rules the legal profession and relatives by marriage.

Since the ninth house has much in common with the ninth zodiacal sign, it takes on many of the attributes of Sagittarius. It is also called the *diurnal house* of Jupiter.

Although the ninth house is cadent, and therefore one of the weakest by house position, its elevation in the horoscope gives it more strength than the other cadent houses to planets found there. Physically it rules the thighs and, to a lesser extent, some parts of the nervous system.

HOUSE X

The TENTH HOUSE is the **House of Ambition** as it rules worldly activities, the native's occupation or profession, his honor, attainments, rank, and fame (or ill-fame), as well as his influence over those with whom he is in contact. It rules the parent of the same sex as the native, except when Leo is on the cusp, when it indicates the father (see house IV).

This house rules governmental affairs and business affairs in general. It is the natural home of the zodiacal sign Capricorn and is called the *natural house* of Saturn, but the ancients considered it the *nocturnal house* of this planet. Being on the Zenith (MC) arm of the Horoscope Cross, it is the highest angular house and planets in it are thus very strong by house position. Physically it rules the knees (especially), the skeleton (in general), the hair, skin, and fingernails.

HOUSE XI

The ELEVENTH HOUSE rules the native's social aspirations, his friends, counselors, and companions. It is the key to his personality as it indicates his attitude toward others and his ability to make and maintain friendships.

Since Aquarius is the natural zodiacal ruler of the house, it takes on some of the Aquarian attributes. It is called the *natural house* of Uranus, but the ancients considered it the *diurnal house* of Saturn.

The eleventh house is succedent and planets found therein are less strong by house position than those in angular houses. Physically this house has rulership over the ankles, lower leg, and total circulation of the blood.

HOUSE XII

The TWELFTH HOUSE, the third and last of the unfortunate houses rules the unseen and unexpected troubles of life, confinement and restraint in hospitals or prisons, or even confinement in the home, (and also employment in an institution such as a hospital or prison, school, etc.). It indicates inhibiting influences of all kinds: seclusion, self-undoing, secret sorrows, silent sufferings, treachery, persecution, and secret enemies. The limitations imposed by this house has been known to lead to suicide. It also rules the occult and hidden phases of life. As the sixth house rules small and domestic animals, so the twelfth house rules large and wild animals.

Pisces, the last sign of the zodiac, finds its natural home in this last house of the horoscope which therefore takes on many Piscean attributes. It is called the *natural house* of Neptune and, by the ancients, the *nocturnal house* of Jupiter. It is the last of the cadent houses, planets in it being weak by house position. Physically it rules the feet and is associated with the endocrine system.

This is the basic information on the houses of the natal horoscope and is one of the three pillars of the astrological structure.

The student is urged to study the lessons carefully, reasoning out the problems in their own fashion, and thinking through the method. Success in astrology requires development of an astrological sense, and the author earnestly hopes that each student will become proficient in this respect by the completion of this course of study.

While astrology has certain fundamental rules, it is more than a science. It is an art, meaning that the astrologer is sometimes left to his or her own resources when hard and fast rules cannot be adduced. Through clinical practice the material in these chapters will become second nature. In horoscopy one cannot always give a rule for everything but knowledge attained plus the development of an "astrological sense" will prove accurate. Experience is a great instructor.

Review Questions for Chapter 2

1. Name and explain the four sciences concerned with the phenomena of the celestial bodies.

2. What branch of astrology do you feel would be most useful to you? And why?

3. Name and discuss the houses of the horoscope.

4. What is a quadrant?

5. Explain the terms Ascendant, Descendant, Midheaven, and Nadir. What is their special importance in the nativity?

6. What is the House of Marriage?

7. Define the difference between Geocentric and Heliocentric motion of the solar system.

|Chapter 3|

Signs of the Zodiac

In addition to the twelve houses discussed in Chapter 2, there is another twelve-fold division of the horoscope circle. This is the division into the twelve signs of the zodiac.

In reality, there are two zodiacs which should not be confused with one another: the **Zodiac of Signs** and the **Constellations**. The latter consists of the actual constellations or groups of fixed stars, of unequal length, which appear in the heavens within about 8 degrees of the line of the ecliptic. See Figure 6 for the generation of the ecliptic. The movement through space of the entire solar system causes these constellations of fixed stars to appear to move backward, approximately 1 degree every 72 years, through the zodiac of signs. This is termed the **Precession**

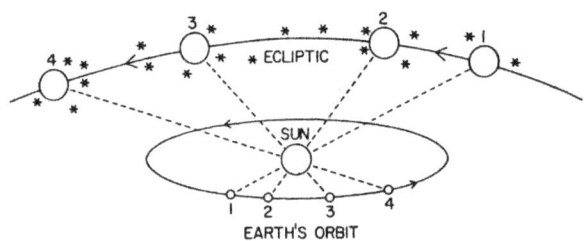

Figure 6. Generation of the ecliptic. As Earth moves around the Sun, the Sun's image appears to be projected on various star groups. The path of the Sun is defined as the ecliptic.

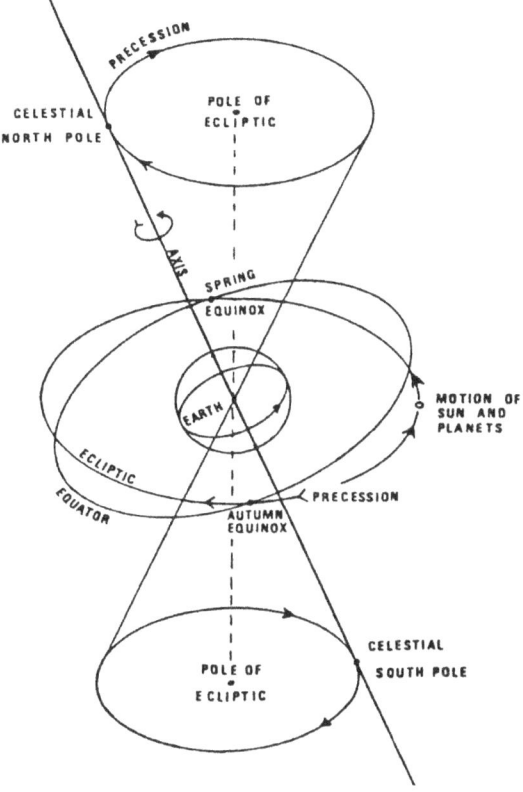

Figure 7. Precession of the equinoxes. The equatorial North Pole is the celestial North Pole as seen from Earth. This apparent pole revolves around the ecliptical North Pole over a period of approximately 26,000 years, sometimes called the Great Year. Our present North Polar Star is Polaris. In 14,000 A.D. it will be Vega.

of the Equinoxes (see Figure 7). The student has no immediate need for this knowledge, however, and for the present need only concern himself with the zodiac of signs, usually referred to in astrology simply as the **Zodiac**.

The apparent annual path of the Sun relative to the stars is called the **Ecliptic**. It is not parallel to the earth's equator,

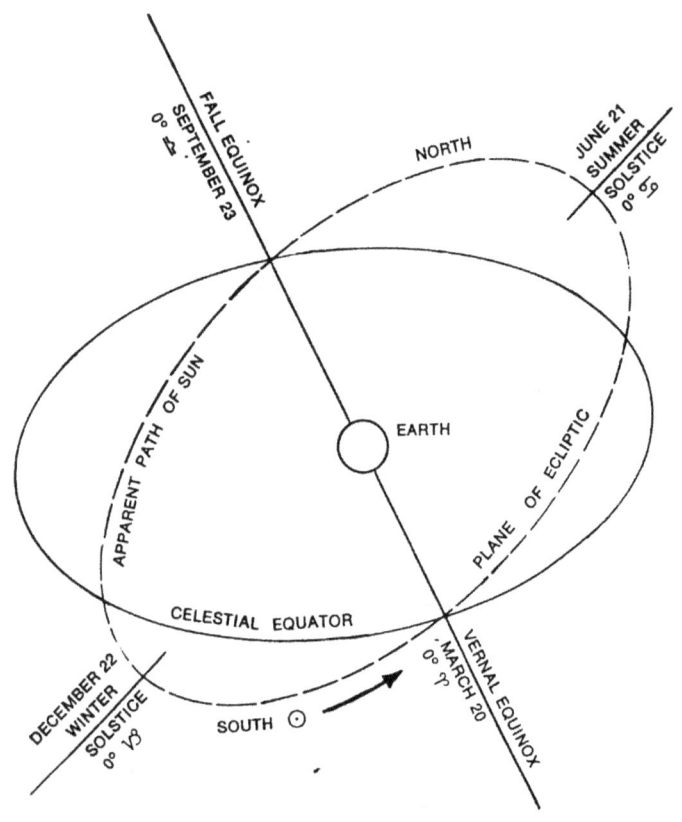

Figure 8. The plane of the ecliptic upon which lies the orbits of the planets, the Sun, and the Moon in their apparent motion as seen from Earth. Shown also are the Vernal Equinox, the Winter Solstice, the Summer Solstice, and the Autumnal or Fall Equinox.

but lies at an angle of approximately 23 degrees and 27 minutes to it; hence the Sun appears to cross the equator twice a year; about March 21, when spring starts in the northern hemisphere, and about September 21, when fall starts in the northern hemisphere.

The zodiac of signs, about 15 degrees to 18 degrees wide

lies along the ecliptic and in it are found all the apparent orbits of the planets as well as the path of the Moon around Earth. The zodiac of signs consists of twelve equal divisions of this space along the ecliptic. Since the zodiac forms a circle, it has no real beginning or end. The tropical zodiac, however, is conventionally measured from the point (taken as 0° Aries) where the Sun crosses the Celestial Equator at the Vernal Equinox (about March 21).[19] Each 30 degrees from Zero degrees Aries marks the beginning of a new sign of the zodiac and is the position of the Sun for each successive month (i.e. each successive twelfth) of the annual apparent path from its passage across the Celestial Equator at the Vernal Equinox back to that same position. (see Figure 8)

The sidereal zodiac, not used in this course, takes its origin from a fixed star relationship in the constellations.

The apparent movement of the Sun from south declination to north declination, (declination is the distance from the equator) is due to the angle between the earth's axis and the plane of its orbit around the Sun. This phenomenon produces the four seasons. Spring commences at the Vernal Equinox, about March 21, when the Sun crosses the Earth's equator, passing from south to north declination, and enters Aries. Three months later, when the Sun appears to have reached its northernmost point of declination and again turns south, it is at 0 Cancer, having passed through the zodiacal signs Aries, Taurus, and Gemini. In another three months, about September 21, the Sun again crosses the equator from north to south declination and enters the zodiacal sign Libra, at the Autumnal Equinox. During this period the Sun has apparently passed through the zodiacal signs Cancer, Leo, and Virgo, Then, when the Sun reaches its furthermost point of southern declination, about December 21, it enters the zodiacal sign Capricorn, and the winter season starts. In the meantime the Sun appears to have passed through the zodiacal signs Libra, Scorpio, and Sagittarius. The Sun then appears to turn northward in its course and passes through the zodiacal

Table 1 Twelve signs of the zodiac

Sign	Associated House	Symbol
Aries	I	The Ram
Taurus	II	The Bull
Gemini	III	The Twins
Cancer	IV	The Crab
Leo	V	The Lion
Virgo	VI	The Virgin
Libra	VII	The Scales (Balance)
Scorpio	VIII	The Scorpion
Sagittarius	IX	The Centaur
Capricorn	X	The Goat
Aquarius	XI	The Water Bearer
Pisces	XII	The Fishes

signs Capricorn, Aquarius, and Pisces until on March 21 of the following year it again reaches Zero degree Aries. In the southern hemisphere the seasons are reversed.

While on the earth's surface, distance north or south of the terrestrial equator is termed latitude, in celestial geography it is termed **Declination. Celestial Latitude** is distance from the plane of the ecliptic.

The twelve signs of the zodiac, their *natural* house rulerships, and their symbols, are shown in Table 1.

Table 1 Twelve signs of the zodiac

Since the Sun is the center of the solar system, with all planets revolving around it, time is measured by the apparent motion of the Sun. But the planets, while following the approximate path of the Sun in the zodiac, move at different speeds. The luminaries and planets move through the signs from west to east, but since the signs themselves appear to be moving from east to west (due to the earth's rotation) the planets thus appear to move from east to west.

Experimental investigation has shown that the zodiacal signs are **Ruled** by the following planets or luminaries:

Sign	Ruler	Sign	Ruler
Aries	Mars	Libra	Venus
Taurus	Venus	Scorpio	Pluto/Mars
Gemini	Mercury	Sagittarius	Jupiter
Cancer	Moon	Capricorn	Saturn
Leo	Sun	Aquarius	Uranus/Saturn
Virgo	Mercury/Asteroids	Pisces	Neptune/Jupiter

The ancients ascribed rulership of Aquarius and Pisces to Saturn and Jupiter, but investigations done since the discovery of Uranus in 1781 and Neptune in 1846 have shown that the former is in its greatest harmony in Aquarius and the latter in Pisces. Since rulership of a sign is indicated by the harmony or affinity of the celestial body for the sign, these two planets have definitely been assigned to Aquarius and Pisces. However, the student should consider Saturn and Jupiter as co–rulers of these signs. Investigations done since the discovery of Pluto in 1930 seem to make this planet ruler of Scorpio, even though the ancients definitely assigned Mars to this sign. There is still controversy on this point, however, with some researchers regarding Pluto as more a ruler of Aries. At present, most American astrologers accept Pluto as ruler, with Mars as co–ruler, of the sign of Scorpio.

THE QUADRUPLICITIES

There are three principal groupings of the signs: (1) the quadruplicities or qualities of action; (2) the triplicities or planes of action; and (3) the trinities, or directions of action.

The signs located naturally on the angles (cusps of houses I, IV, VII and X) are called CARDINAL SIGNS because they indicate activity or outward-directed action. These signs are Aries, Cancer, Libra, and Capricorn and the student will note that the onset of each marks a change in the apparent direction of the Sun (in the ecliptic) in relation to the earth. These are the forceful, energetic, and enterprising signs. When well aspected, they furnish the native with ambition, enthusiasm, and drive, i.e., the degree of forcefulness needed for success in life. They are progressive. When afflicted, they indicate a restless and inconstant busybody, always unsettled and never completing any task. These signs are always active; leaders and pioneers invariably have them prominent in their horoscopes.

The natural rulers of houses II, V, VIII, and XI, Taurus, Leo, Scorpio, and Aquarius are the FIXED SIGNS. Stability is their keynote, as they fix or stabilize opinions and habits plus supplying stamina and persistence. The native has an analytical mind and is dogmatic and unyielding, but when convinced or changed becomes as strongly attached to the new position as he was to the old. Persons of settled habits and those in administrative positions usually have these signs prominent. When afflicted, they are stubborn, bullheaded, and proud.

The third group of quadruplicities are the MUTABLE SIGNS, indicating adaptability. These are the natural rulers of houses III, VI, IX and XII, Gemini, Virgo, Sagittarius, and Pisces. While very flexible, they also confer intellectual impartiality; judgment is passed only when all the facts have been carefully weighed. In the case of Gemini, however, there is sometimes a tendency to jump to conclusions, this being due mainly to the nervous temperament and active mind of the native. These signs usually produce artists and students: while fickle, they still seek expression through thought. The moral, intellectual, and spiritual qualities are found here. Mediators, students, inventors, scientists, and philosophers generally have these signs prominent, as well as writers, journalists, mathematicians, and artists. When afflicted, they diffuse their mental and physical energies, with resultant superficiality in all of their undertakings.

THE TRIPLICITIES

The next division of the signs is into **Triplicities**, representing the four elements of matter known to the ancients: FIRE, EARTH, AIR, and WATER.

The first, fifth, and ninth signs, (Aries, Leo, and Sagittarius) represent the fiery element. Their plane of action is essentially mental: when well aspected they give stamina and vitality but when negatively configured produce fevers and inflammatory disorders. They are forceful and positive, conferring self-confidence. While largely spiritual in character, the fire signs also confer inexhaustible energy and excite continuous activity. The dynamic personality of these signs, when well aspected, is apparent to all with whom they come into contact. The key to their nature is FIRE.

The second, sixth and tenth signs, (Taurus, Virgo, and Capricorn) represent the earthy element. Their plane of action is physical and the materialistic side of life predominates. They control the environment and bestow wonderful recuperative powers. These signs are largely responsible for the so–called inferiority complex as they inhibit the native's self expression. This is a limiting factor and reduces the native to the sole realm of practicality, sometimes going so far as to cause melancholy. The key to their nature is EARTH.

The third, seventh, and eleventh signs, (Gemini, Libra, and Aquarius) represent the airy element. Their plane of action is intuitional, and here we find the attachments of life: brethren, partners, and friends.

When well aspected, these signs confer versatility and a personality which blends happily with others. When badly aspected, the native is verbose and impractical. This is the most errant and most difficult to control element. Persons of nervous temperament usually have these signs predominating. The key to their nature is AIR.

The fourth, eighth, and twelfth signs, (Cancer, Scorpio, and Pisces) rule the last of the elements, water. Their plane of action is emotional, and here is the complement of fire, which produces the fearful, shrinking, self-protective individual. Yet these persons can adjust to any occasion, just as water fits itself into any vessel. An emotional temperament, changeable in the extreme, typifies the person in whom the watery signs predominate. Altruistic and profound, they concern themselves much with divine and natural law, often to their own detriment. When badly aspected, there is a tendency to worry, usually about matters which will probably never happen. They are easily influenced and moody in the extreme. The key to their nature is WATER.

The foregoing divisions of the elements has been exposited since ancient times and still hold, yet some research has been done on dividing the elements into six classes. A Scottish Astro–researcher, Maurice Wemyss[20] has postulated the following categories: **Electricity** for Aries and Libra, **Crystalline** for Taurus and Scorpio, **Energy** for Gemini and Sagittarius. **Solids** for Cancer and Capricorn, **Gasses** for Leo and Aquarius, and **Liquids** for Virgo and Pisces. The arguments in favor of these divisions will require a long period of research before usage would be practical.

THE TRINITIES

The third division of the zodiacal signs into four groups is called the **Trinities**. The first of these, comprising Aries, Taurus, and Gemini, is known as the INTELLECTUAL TRINITY. The second group comprises Cancer, Leo, and Virgo, and is known as the MATERNAL TRINITY. The third group includes Libra, Scorpio, and Sagittarius, and is the REPRODUCTIVE TRINITY. The fourth group is made up of Capricorn, Aquarius, and

Table 2. The signs of the zodiac with their quality, plane, and mode of action as:

Zodiac Sign	Quadruplicity Quality of Action	Triplicity Plane of Action	Trinity Mode of Action	Receptivity	Direction or Ecliptic
Aries ♈	Cardinal	Fire	Intellectual	+	Northern
Taurus ♉	Fixed	Earth	Intellectual	−	Northern
Gemini ♊	Mutable	Air	Intellectual	+	Northern
Cancer ♋	Cardinal	Water	Maternal	−	Northern
Leo ♌	Fixed	Fire	Maternal	+	Northern
Virgo ♍	Mutable	Earth	Maternal	−	Northern
Libra ♎	Cardinal	Air	Reproductive	+	Southern
Scorpio ♏	Fixed	Water	Reproductive	−	Southern
Sagittarius ♐	Mutable	Fire	Reproductive	+	Southern
Capricorn ♑	Cardinal	Earth	Serving	−	Southern
Aquarius ♒	Fixed	Air	Serving	+	Southern
Pisces ♓	Mutable	Water	Serving	−	Southern

Pisces, and is known as the SERVING TRINITY.

It should be borne in mind that the quadruplicities are the qualities of action, the triplicities are the planes of action, and the trinities are the modes of action. In judging a horoscope it is necessary to consider the grouping of the planets in all of these divisions. (see Table 2)

DIRECTION

Two other divisions of the signs of the zodiac are sometimes of major importance. The first is the division into ASCENDING and DESCENDING (northern and southern) SIGNS. Aries, Taurus, Gemini, Cancer, Leo, and Virgo are the ascending signs indicating personal effort in behalf of self. Libra, Scorpio, Sagittarius, Capricorn, Aquarius, and Pisces are descending signs and indicate personal effort in relation to others.

RECEPTIVITY

The second is a division into POSITIVE (active) and NEGATIVE (receptive) SIGNS. The odd-numbered signs (Ar-

Signs of short ascension December 21:	Signs of long ascension June 21:
Capricorn	Cancer
Aquarius	Leo
Pisces	Virgo
Aries - March 21	Libra - September 21
Taurus	Scorpio
Gemini	Sagittarius

Figure 9. A diagram of the ecliptic showing signs of short ascension, Capricorn through Gemini, and signs of long ascension, Cancer through Sagittarius.

ies, Gemini, Leo, Libra, Sagittarius, and Aquarius) are positive and masculine, or assertive. The even-numbered Signs (Taurus, Cancer, Virgo, Scorpio, Capricorn, and Pisces) are negative and feminine, or receptive.

The signs of long ascension occur when the rising Sun is more parallel to the celestial equator; in the northern hemisphere these are generally the signs Cancer through Sagittarius. The signs of short ascension are Capricorn through Gemini. (see Figure 9.)

THE INDIVIDUAL SIGNS

The student should carefully read and reread the foregoing, learning the symbol for each sign. While the materials need not be memorized verbatim, the fundamentals set forth should be firmly fixed in the mind. The following adjectives associated with the individual signs of the zodiac should also be learned.

ARIES is a northern, masculine, fiery, cardinal, positive, violent, bestial sign of short ascension. It is the first sign of the intellectual trinity, the cardinal quadruplicity, and the fiery triplicity. It is ruled by the planet Mars.

TAURUS is a northern, feminine, earthy, fixed, negative, fruitful, bestial, sign of short ascension. It is the second sign of the intellectual trinity, the first sign of the fixed quadruplicity, and of the earthy triplicity. It is ruled by the planet Venus.

GEMINI is a northern, masculine, airy, common, positive, vocal, human, barren, double-bodied sign of short ascension. It is the third sign of the intellectual trinity, the first sign of the mutable quadruplicity, and of the airy triplicity. It is ruled by the planet Mercury.

CANCER is a northern feminine, watery, cardinal, negative, mute, reptilian, fruitful sign of long ascension. It is the first sign of the maternal trinity and of the watery triplicity but the second sign of the cardinal quadruplicity. It is ruled by the Moon.

LEO is a northern, masculine, fiery, positive, fixed, bestial, barren sign of long ascension. It is the second sign of the maternal trinity and of the fixed quadruplicity as well as of the fiery triplicity. It is ruled by the Sun.

VIRGO is a northern, feminine, negative, earthy ,common, human, barren sign of long ascension. It is the third sign of the maternal trinity but the second sign of the mutable quadruplicity and the earthy triplicity. It is ruled by the planet Mercury, although some contemporary astrologers give the rulership to the asteroid belt.

LIBRA is a southern, masculine, positive, airy, cardinal, vocal sign of long ascension. It is the first sign of the reproductive trinity, the second sign of the airy triplicity, and the third sign of the cardinal quadruplicity. As it is the opposite of Aries, it is complementary to Aries. It is ruled by the planet Venus.

SCORPIO is a southern, feminine, watery, fixed, negative, violent, fruitful, mute, reptilian sign of long ascension. It is the second sign of the reproductive trinity and the third sign of the fixed quadruplicity as well as the second sign of the watery triplicity. As it is the opposite of Taurus, it is complementary to Taurus. Scorpio is co–ruled by Pluto and Mars.

SAGITTARIUS is a southern, masculine, positive, fiery, common, half- human, and half-bestial sign of long ascension. It is the third sign of the reproductive trinity, and mutable quadruplicity, and the fiery triplicity. It is ruled by the planet Jupiter.

CAPRICORN is a southern, feminine, negative, earthy, cardinal, bestial, violent sign of short ascension. It is the third sign of the earthy triplicity, the fourth sign of the cardinal quadruplicity, and the first sign of the serving trinity. It is ruled by the planet Saturn.

AQUARIUS is a southern, masculine, positive, airy, fixed, vocal, human sign of short ascension. It is the second sign of the serving trinity, the third sign of the airy triplicity, and the fourth sign of the fixed quadruplicity. It is ruled by the planet Uranus, although Saturn is considered as a co–ruler.

PISCES is a southern, feminine, negative, watery, common, mute, fruitful, reptilian, double-bodied sign of short ascension. It is the third sign of the serving trinity and the watery triplicity as well as the fourth sign of the mutable quadruplicity. It is ruled by the planet Neptune, although Jupiter is considered as a co–ruler.

Review Questions for Chapter 3

1. What is the difference between the Zodiac of Signs and the Zodiac of Constellations? How does this account for the present idea of the Age of Aquarius?

2. List the signs of the zodiac with their symbols and house connections.

3. What is meant by the quadruplicities being qualities of action?

4. Group the zodiac signs according to their elements or planes of action.

5. Under what signs of the zodiac will you find most inventors and scientists? Under which signs will you expect musicians and poets?

6. What zodiac signs show leadership ability?

7. Describe in your own words the masculine and feminine expression of the various signs.

|CHAPTER 4|

Celestial Bodies

In the zodiac of signs all planets revolve around the Sun, with their apparent orbits lying along the path of the Sun (the ecliptic), and all falling within the zodiac whose width is about 15 to 18 degrees of space. The period required by each planet for a complete revolution in its orbit is called a Planetary Year. Table 3 gives the approximate time taken by each planet for one complete revolution (the earth's year being taken as the standard of measurement), the mean distance of each from the Sun, and the approximate diameter of each body:

Table 3. Major planets of this solar system.

Planet	Planetary Year or Solar Orbital Revolution (approximate)	Equatorial Diameter (in miles)	Mean Distance from Sun (in millions of miles)
Mercury	88 days	3,025	36
Venus	224.7 days	7,526	67
Earth	365.26 days	7,927	93
Mars	687 days	4,218	141
Asteroids	4.6 years	varies	260
Jupiter	11.86 years	88,700	483
Saturn	29.46 years	75,100	886
Uranus	84.01 years	29,200	1,782
Neptune	164.8 years	31,650	2,792
Pluto	247.7 years	3,550	3,664

Neptune and Pluto were sought by astronomers once their existence and positions had been foretold by astrologers and calculated by mathematical astronomy. Uranus, Neptune, and Pluto, discovered in 1782, 1846, and 1930, respectively, were, of course, not used by the ancients as planets of the solar system if their existence was known at all. Astronomers believe that another trans–Neptunian planet exists, probably more distant than Pluto, while many research astrologers believe that still others will be discovered.

The planetoids, or asteroids as they are generally called, are the parts of a disintegrated planet; most of their orbits lying between Mars and Jupiter, about 200–400 million miles from the Sun. Their influence is unknown, although their largest bodies are considered in some methods of astrology.[22]

One other celestial body, however, which plays a major role in astrology because of its tremendous influence on things terrestrial is the earth's satellite, the Moon. It makes a complete revolution around the earth in the lunar month of 27 days, 7 hours, and 43 minutes. The Moon is approximately 239,000 miles from the earth, being its closest neighbor in the heavens, and has a diameter of about 2,162 miles.

NATURE OF THE PLANETS AND LUMINARIES

The Sun and Moon, known collectively as the luminaries, and each of the planets has its own specific nature which varies in strength according to its position in the heavens – either by sign position, house position, or geometrical relationship (aspect) to the positions of other celestial bodies, especially those of the solar system. The planet naturally has its greatest strength when in a sign with which its own nature harmonizes, when it is said to be in dignity. It is always referred to as the ruler of that sign.

Planets are also found to harmonize to a lesser degree with certain other signs; when found in them the planets are said to be exalted, because this harmony increases the force of the planet as well as its virtues.

A planet is said to be in its detriment when found in the sign opposite to the one it rules because its environment is then not in harmony with its natural characteristics but, instead, is in opposition to them.

When a planet is found in the sign opposite its exaltation, it is in its fall, i.e, its most unfortunate astrological position. A person with many planets so posited in his natal horoscope finds life full of disappointments, and a hard uphill fight is needed to overcome these obstacles.

When a planet is dignified or exalted, its benefic influences are magnified.

When in its detriment or fall, its difficult influences are increased.

The SUN rules Leo, is exalted in Aries, is in its detriment in Aquarius, and in its fall in Libra.

The MOON rules Cancer, is exalted in Taurus, is in its detriment in Capricorn, and in its fall in Scorpio.

MERCURY rules Gemini and possibly Virgo, is exalted in Aquarius, is in its detriment in Sagittarius and Pisces, and in its fall in Leo.

VENUS rules Taurus and Libra, is exalted in Pisces, in its detriment in Scorpio and Aries, and in its fall in Virgo.

MARS rules Aries and Scorpio, is exalted in Capricorn, in its detriment in Libra and Taurus, and in its fall in Cancer.

JUPITER rules Sagittarius, is exalted in Cancer, in its detriment in Gemini, and in its fall in Capricorn.

SATURN rules Capricorn, is exalted in Libra, in its detriment in Cancer, and its fall in Aries.

URANUS rules Aquarius, is exalted in Scorpio, in its detriment in Leo, and its fall in Taurus.

NEPTUNE rules Pisces, is exalted in Sagittarius, in its detriment in Virgo, and its fall in Gemini.

PLUTO rules Scorpio and Aries, is exalted in Leo , in its detriment in Taurus and Libra and its fall in Aquarius.

Table 4. Planets of the solar system with the zodiac signs in which they have their rulerships, falls, exaltations and detriments.

Planets	Symbols	Rule	Detriment	Exaltation	Fall
Sun	☉	♌	♒	♈	♎
Moon	☽	♋	♑	♉	♏
Mercury	☿	♊ ♍	♐ ♓	♒	♌
Venus	♀	♉ ♎	♏ ♈	♓	♍
Mars	♂	♈	♎	♑	♋
Jupiter	♃	♐	♊	♋	♑
Saturn	♄	♑	♋	♎	♈
Uranus	♅	♒	♌	♏	♉
Neptune	♆	♓	♍	♐	♊
Pluto	♇	♏	♉	♌	♒

The student cannot be urged too strongly to learn Table 4 carefully and thoroughly, for it is information of the greatest importance for astrology. When these general data have been thoroughly mastered, the student should memorize the following specific characteristics of each planet:

The SUN, ruler of Leo and the source of all life in the solar system, is a male, fixed, fiery, benefic planet,[23] full of vigor and by nature rather fruitful. It is executive, truthful, masterful, and creative. The Sun is the source of the native's individuality.

The MOON rules the sign Cancer and is cold, moist, phlegmatic, and feminine in character. Benefic in its influence, it is cardinal, receptive, and magnetic, but also wandering and changeable. It stimulates the imagination, the instincts, and the humanitarian qualities. The Moon is so fruitful that it is frequently called the planet of fecundity. It is very sympathetic and stimulates the higher emotional faculties. Just as the Sun confers the native's individuality, so the Moon is the source of his personality which is the outward expression or reflection of his individuality.

MERCURY, the ruler of Gemini and Virgo, is a mutable intellectual planet, quick, volatile, and uncertain, and with a variable nature. It is active, nervous, and excitable, but also self-expressive, thoughtful, eloquent, and affable. It is a cold, moist planet and moderately fruitful. Mercury takes on the nature of the planets to which it is most strongly aspected and for that reason is often called the Messenger of the Gods. It has to do with the concrete mental faculties and is the source of the mentality in the same sense that the Sun and Moon are the sources of the individuality and personality.

VENUS rules the zodiac signs Taurus and Libra. Its nature is harmony, adaptability, idealism, love, and gentility. Its influence is so benefic that it is called the lesser benefic (Jupiter being the greater benefic). Venus is graceful, magnetic, and pacific, as well as social, imaginative, and of a fertile mind. It is the planet of contentment, being passive, warm, moist, and fruitful.

The fiery, dynamic MARS rules Aries and is co–ruler of Scorpio, producing unbounded energy and physical activity. It is a quick, positive, electric, forceful, hot, dry, and barren planet. While Mars is sometimes termed the lesser malefic (Saturn being the greater malefic), its action is positive. It typifies great courage.

The greater benefic is JUPITER, which rules the sign Sagittarius and, with Neptune, is co–ruler of Pisces. Jupiter is mutable, moral, fiery, and benevolent, bestowing a generous, genial, orderly, temperate, and healthy influence in all its relationships. It is of the higher scale of Venus and, while not so magnetic, is positive, hot, moist, and fruitful. Jupiter's high aspirations produce great hope.

SATURN rules the zodiac sign Capricorn and, with Uranus, is co–ruler of Aquarius. Its stern limiting qualities cause it to be termed the major malefic. It is cautious, slow, thorough, and inevitable in its influence, as well as negative, nervous, and secretive. Saturn is the great teacher, cautioning prudence in every undertaking.

URANUS, ruler of Aquarius, is the planet of invention, originality, versatility, and progressive ideals. While it has the energy of fire and the emotion of water, it is cold and barren, spasmodic and separative, as well as drastic in influence. It always produces the unexpected in a sudden manner. It has a variable nature but is magnetic and electric. The influence of Uranus is basically mental, thus it is termed the higher octave of Mercury. It is a major malefic influence, as man measures values, but usually bestows more than it takes away. The originality of Uranus is best illustrated by the trend of the present age of invention of things electrical, mechanical, and aerial; also by the spasmodic changes occurring in civilization generally at the present time, over which period of the earth's history Uranus holds rule.

NEPTUNE, the ruler of Pisces, is highly emotional and subtle in influence, as well as delicate, aesthetic, moist, and warm. It is also highly musical. Neptune has been considered malefic in character, but this is probably due to our incomplete understanding of it and inability to attune life to its high vibrations. While its influence is negative, characterized by unfulfilled promise, it is a planet of great inspiration or degradation, running to these extremes. It has much to do with occult science. Neptune is passive in nature, and those whose charts it dominates are difficult to understand. This planet is considered to be the higher octave of magnetic Venus.

PLUTO rules the watery sign of Scorpio along with its co-ruler Mars. This newest member of the solar system both binds and loosens as it seeks to blend diverse units into a singleness.

Though Pluto may seem to bring death and upheaval it builds anew out of the ashes of the old. Like the phoenix symbol to which Pluto is often compared this planet brings transformations of one force upon another. Considered as a turning point, Pluto can be seen as a connection or transition force much like a bridge between two boundaries. It is a small, dense hard–hitting planet with great persistence. Pluto has a close relationship with Jupiter although it is considered to represent a higher octave of militant Mars.

Other celestial bodies beyond the solar system are the fixed stars, the zodiac of constellations, star clusters, comets, etc, but the student need not at present concern himself with them. They are discussed generally in Chapter 9.

Chapters 2, 3, and 4 have set forth the fundamental nature of the houses, the signs of the zodiac, and the planets. Although other factors as well are considered in horoscopy, these are the foundations of all astrological science. Once the horoscope has been calculated, it must be interpreted, and this depends on a thorough understanding of these natures. They are not only to be learned, they must become second nature, as this will develop the "astrological sense" which is essential to a correct delineation of horoscopes.

At the present stage, however, the student should read these chapters over several times with a view, not to memorizing them verbatim but to understanding principles, gaining perspective, and learning symbols. A list of additional reading material is provided below:

Recommended Titles:

- Arroyo, Stephen, *Chart Interpretation Handbook*, Sebastopol, CA, CRCS Publications
- Clement, Stephanie Jean, PhD, *Mapping Your Birth Chart*, St Paul, MN, 2003
- Dobyns, Zipporah, PhD, *Finding the Person in the Horo-*

scope, Tempe, AZ, American Federation of Astrologers, 2012

- George, Llewellyn, *New A-Z Horoscope Maker and Delineator*, Woodbury, MN, 1980
- Hand, Robert, *Horoscope Symbols*, Rockport, MA, Para Research 1981
- Herring, Amy, *Essential Astrology*, Llewellyn Publications, Woodbury, MN, 2017
- Jones, Marc Edmund, *Astrology: How and Why it Works*, Boulder, CO, Shambhala Publications, 1945
- Mann, Mark, *Astrology for the Absolute Beginner*, Eugene, OR, Breakthrough Enterprises, 1995
- Marks, Tracy, *The Art of Chart Interpretation*, Lake Worth, FL, Ibis Press, 2009
- Sakoian, Frances and Acker, Louis, *Astrologer's Handbook*, New York, Harper and Rowe, 1973

Review Questions for Chapter 4

1. Prepare a table of the rulerships, exaltations, detriments, and falls of the ten major planets and luminaries.

2. How would you compare the expressions of Venus and Mars? Also of Saturn and Jupiter?

3. Show how the luminaries complement and balance each other in their total, combined expression.

4. Which planets have been discovered in the past 300 years?

Chapter 5

Calculating the Horoscope

A HOROSCOPE IS SIMPLY A CHART of the ecliptic in relationship to a given place on the earth at a certain moment, showing the longitudinal positions of the Sun, Moon and planets. If it were not for two astrological publications – Ephemerides and Tables of Houses – it would be necessary for the student to have knowledge of spherical trigonometry and, by complicated formulae, calculate the positions of the celestial bodies for the moment of birth.

The ephemeris is a statistical publication giving the longitude, latitude and declinations of the luminaries and each planet, with the relative sidereal (star) time. Usually, it is calculated for noon or midnight at Greenwich, England.[24]

The table of houses is a permanent publication giving the position of the zodiac on each house cusp for the various degrees of terrestrial latitude, at stated sidereal times throughout the 24 hours. AFA Placidus System, Rosicrucian Tables of Houses and the Michelson Book of Tables are each calculated for every degree of the zodiac on the midheaven. All of these tables of houses are based on the Placidus system of intermediate house division, which is currently the most popular and commonly found system of house division.[25] The Michelson Book of Tables features both Placidus and Koch house divisions.

No long technical terms are used in this course of instruction unless absolutely necessary, as it is designed to simplify the calculation of the horoscope for the student. In those instances where technical terms are unavoidable, definitions will be given. The course itself is intended to reduce all mathematical calculations to the simplest possible degree consistent with good astrological practice and accuracy for ordinary work.

The student will remember that there are three predominant factors in the calculation of each horoscope: the houses, the signs of the zodiac, and the planets. In Chapter 2, it was learned that the houses never change their positions (see Figure 5, Chapter 2). They remain constant and are always the same in every horoscope erected by the fixed Ascendant method.

The zodiac, however, is constantly changing due to the rotation of Earth, and this rotation, plus the movement of each of the planets in its orbit through the zodiac around the Sun causes them also to change their positions. This accounts for the fact that no two horoscopes can be alike unless persons are born at the same moment in the same place. But it should be remembered that the signs of the zodiac always maintain their regular sequence in counter-clockwise order beginning with Aries and ending with Pisces.

CALCULATING THE HOROSCOPE

The first step in creating the horoscope chart is to calculate the relative position of the zodiac to the place of birth at the moment of birth. The elements entering into this equation are the time and place of birth. Time is relative; it is man's measurement of the sequence of events. The ordinary time in use today throughout almost all of the civilized world is based on Greenwich corrected or Universal Time.[26]

In the United States and Canada there are ten different standard time zones. They are: Atlantic Standard Time; Newfoundland Standard Time; Eastern Standard Time; Central Standard Time; Mountain Standard Time; Pacific Standard Time; Yukon Standard Time; Alaskan Standard Time; Hawaiian Standard Time; and Bering Standard Time (Table 5 and Figure 10).

Prior to noon of November 18, 1883, every town and city in the United States had a different time from every other, based upon the Sun's position on the meridian of that town at noon. With the development of railroads, telegraph, and national and international means of prompt communication, this brought extreme confusion. The steps taken to overcome this condition resulted in the adoption of Standard Time.

Clock time is measured by the daily rotation of the earth upon its axis, consequently a starting point somewhere upon the earth's surface was necessary for measurement. Greenwich, England, at 0 degrees of longitude, is universally recognized as that starting point.

As the earth rotates once in approximately twenty-four hours, the Sun appears to move 15 degrees of longitude in one hour: 15° x 24 hours = 360°. Therefore, at each 15 degree interval of longitude west of Greenwich, and starting at the 75th meridian in the United States, a standard time zone was established. The result was that the Eastern Standard Time Zone (EST), based on 75 degrees of longitude west of Greenwich, is five hours earlier than the standard time of Greenwich, usually called Greenwich Mean Time, or Universal Time (GMT or UT). At 90°W longitude is the meridian of the Central Standard Time Zone; at 105°W is Mountain Standard Time, and 120°W, is Pacific Standard Time. Likewise each 15 degrees east longitude theoretically marks an hour of standard time.

The midpoint between these meridians is theoretically the changing point for standard time. For example, Eastern Stan-

Standard Time Zone	ST Meridian in Degrees	Difference from GMT in Hours
Greenwich Mean Time (GMT or UT)	0 W/E	0
W Africa (WAT)	15 W	−1
Azores (AT)	30 W	−2
Brazil (Zone 2)	45 W	−3
New Foundland (NST)	52 W 30	−3:30
Atlantic (AST)	60 W	−4
Eastern (EST)	75 W	−5
Central (CST)	90 W	−6
Mountain (MST)	105 W	−7
Pacific (PST)	120 W	−8
Yukon (YST)	135 W	−9
Alaska/Hawaii (AHST)	150 W	−10
Hawaiian (HST)	157 W 30	−10:30
Bering (Samoa) (BST)	165 W	−11
International Date Line	180 W/E	−12
New Zealand (NZT	180 E	+12
Guam (GST)	150 E	+10
South Australia (SAST)	142 E 30	+9:30
Japan (JST)	135 E	+9
China Coast (CCT)	120 E	+8
Java (JT)	112 E	+7:30
South Sumatra (SST)	105 E	+7
North Sumatra (NST)	97 E 30	+6:30
No agreed name (Zone 5)	90 E	+6
Indian (IST)	82 E 30	+5:30
No agreed name (Zone 4)	75 E	+5
No agreed name (Zone 3)	60 E	+4
Baghdad (BAT)	45 E	+3
Eastern European (EET)	30 E	+2
Central European Time (CET)	15 E	+1

Table 5. Standard time zones of the world. War Time, Daylight Savings Time, Double Time, etc., must be determined from the records of each of the countries individually.

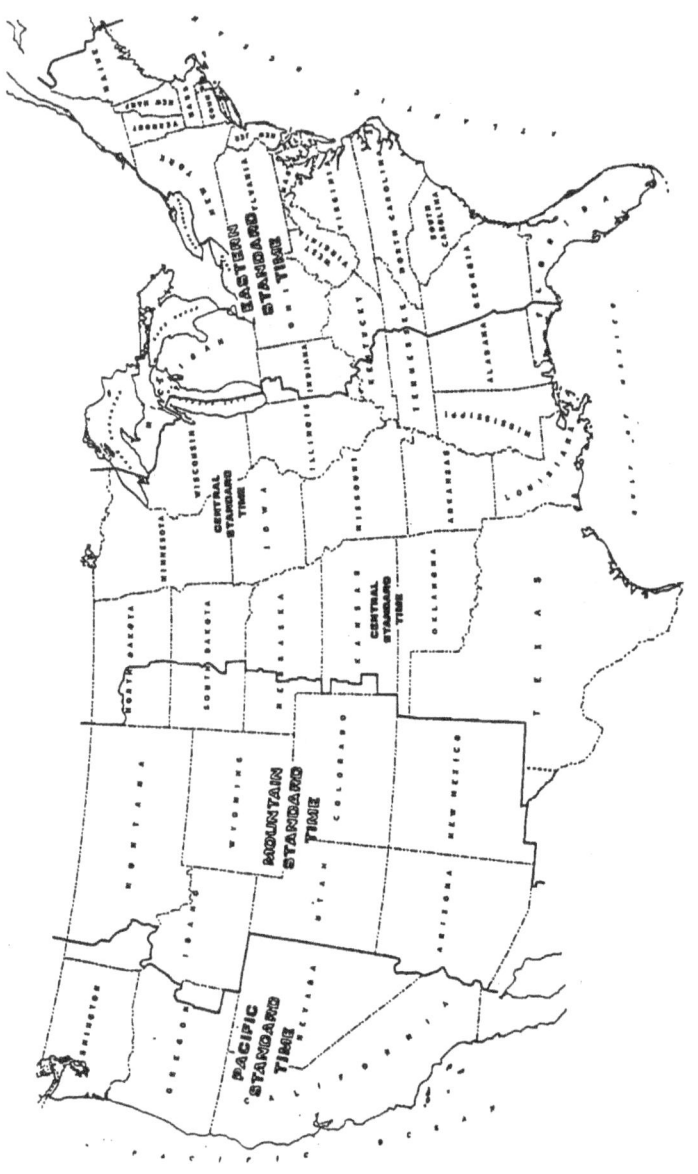

Figure 10. Times zones of the United States.

dard Time theoretically extends from 67°W30' to 82°W30'. In practice, however, there are some exceptions to this rule, as in the case of Detroit, Michigan. Actually, Detroit is 83°W03' and belongs in the Central Standard Time Zone, where it was until 1912, but through state legislation the western limit of the Eastern Standard Time Zone was "bent" around Detroit so that Detroit's time is observed as Eastern Standard Time. Similarly, various changes of this kind were made in Ohio, Georgia, North Dakota, and other states.

War Time

From 2:00 AM on February 2, 1942, to 2:00 AM on September 30,1945, all time (standard) in the United States was advanced one hour and this new time was called War Time. During the first World War clocks were similarly advanced one hour during the summer months and this was called Daylight Savings Time. In some sections of the country, particularly large metropolitan areas, this practice continued. Of course, this one hour must be deducted to arrive at standard time and then correction should be made to ascertain Local Mean Time (LMT). Care must always be exercised in obtaining birth data to know what kind of time is referred to. This has caused much confusion as many places do not use this Daylight Savings Time, and in some European countries they call it Summer Time. England has also used a Double Daylight Saving Time or two-hour differential. Refer to a book on time changes for local birth time discrepancies.[27]

Sidereal Time

Still another kind of time is used by all astronomers and astrologers, it is called Sidereal Time. Sidereal time is simply star time. Our mean day of 24 hours is based upon the relationships between Earth and Sun, but the sidereal day is the time it takes a fixed star to return successively to the same meridian, while the mean solar day is the time required for the Sun to return successively to the same meridian. The sidereal year and the first sidereal day of that year are measured from the moment of the Vernal Equinox when the Sun crosses the equator, about March 21st of each year, when it also enters the first zodiacal sign, Aries.

Earth rotating on its axis will, in one full rotation, return a fixed star to its beginning meridian in 360 degrees, while the same rotation will bring the Sun to its starting point in approximately 361 degrees. Sidereal time being based on a fixed star rather than on the Sun, the sidereal day increases approximately 4 minutes (1 ° = 4^m) daily in terms of solar time. To put it another way, because the mean solar day (upon which standard time is based) is based on a star (the Sun), which takes almost four minutes longer to return to a meridian than a fixed star, the sidereal day is almost 4 minutes shorter than the mean solar day of 24 hours. Therefore, because the Sun advances almost 1 degree daily (or 360° in 365 ¼ days), the sidereal day advances a full 24 hours in the course of a solar year, beginning again at the Vernal Equinox.

As stated above, the ephemeris gives the sidereal time (ST) for midnight or noon of each day of the year at Greenwich, as well as the positions of the planets, the Sun and Moon, in the zodiac. Remember the position of a celestial body in the zodiac is its LONGITUDE – celestial longitude – or its distance from Aries 0°00'00" in the ecliptic.

*NOTE: What we will present in this lesson is but one method of horoscope calculation. There are many methods of calculation in use, and all of them are valid. The student may use any method with which she or he is more comfortable.

For the purpose of illustrating these factors step by step, lets calculate the horoscope of a female child:

Information required is: the native's birth date (day, month and year), exact time of birth, and the location of birth.

Since the reference material you will use is calculated for sidereal time, midnight, Greenwich, England, you will have to make several adjustments in order to arrive at the correct time of birth. The first adjustment necessary is a time zone adjustment to convert actual time of birth to Greenwich time.

Time Zone adjustments for the United States are as follows:

   A. Eastern Standard Time – Add 5 Hours to birth time to correct the Greenwich time.

   B. Central Standard Time – Add 6 Hours to birth time.

   C. Mountain Standard Time – Add 7 Hours to birth time.

   D. Pacific Standard Time – Add 8 Hours to birth time.

Note: When working with a birth which occurred during Daylight Savings Time, first subtract 1 hour from time of birth, then add the correct zone adjustment.

For instance, let's assume the native was born at 3:36:00 PM, July 20, 1971 Mountain Daylight Time:

   Name: Female Child
   Birth Date: July 20, 1971
   Birth Place: Salt Lake City, Utah, 111°W 53' 25'
                                        40°N 45' 39"

   1) 3:36 PM —Time of birth

   2) – 1:00 =   — Adjust Daylight Time to Standard Time

   3) 2:36 PM — Time of Birth Corrected to Standard Time.

The next step is adjusting for the time zone in which the child was born. Mountain Standard Time occurs seven hours later than Greenwich time, so we must add seven hours of time to the native's birth. Had she been born in the South Sumatra Time Zone, we would have to subtract seven hours of time from the her birth. In the next chapter we will learn more about births east of Greenwich.

    2:36 PM

    4) + 7:00:00 = — Zone Correction to MST.

    5) 9:36 PM or 21:36 hours July 20, 1971

The time of birth has now been adjusted to Greenwich Time. Since this birth occurred after 12:00 noon of July 20, it was during the PM hours, so we had to add 12 hours to the birth time to get the total number of hours that passed since 12:00 Midnight. *Remember – for all births that occurred from 1:00 PM onwards, add 12 hours to the time. Do NOT add 12 hours for any time from 12:00 noon to 12:59 PM, as they will be expressed in this way: 12:59 PM =12 hours and 59 minutes after midnight; 12:30 =12 hours and 30 minutes after midnight. This is like military time which is always given as hours, never AM or PM, thus 10:00 PM is really 22:00 hours regardless of the time zone.

With this adjustment the time is now expressed as: 21:36:00 — The birth occurred 21 hours and 36 minutes after midnight, July 20, 1971. The next step is to calculate the planetary longitudes.

Again, use the method with which you are the most comfortable, as you will be using it repetitiously. This repetition is helpful for the student to memorize the steps.

Calculating the Planetary Longitudes

On the following page you will see a copy of the ephemeris page for July 1971. Our task is to determine how far each planet moved in 21 hours and 36 minutes. To do that we will need to determine the total movement of each heavenly body in a 24 hour period.

Begin by first recording the planetary positions for the day **after** our Female Child was born, July 21, 1971. Remember – we are looking for the total travel time, or daily motion, of all the planets in a 24 hour period, so we subtract the positions for the date in question FROM the following date.

In the case of Mars, Jupiter and Neptune the letters **Rx** follow the longitudes as given in the ephemeris. This indicates that the apparent motion of the planet in question is **retrograde**. Of course, these planets are not really moving backwards, but the positions of Earth and Sun relative to them made them appear to be moving backwards through the zodiac. This is called retrograde motion, and all the planets except the Sun and Moon manifest this apparent motion on a periodic basis. The Sun moves so far ahead of the planets, periodically, that from the Earth they appear to be moving backwards. Both the Moon and Sun appear to travel more rapidly than at other times, but their forward movement is such that they never appear to be retrograde.

Next, record the planetary positions for the birth date, July 20, 1971, and subtract. In the case of retrogrades– and there are three during the dates in question– subtract the lower number from the higher, and record the answer as a negative number. Example:

♂ Rx: 21° 28" July 20

-21° 21' = July 21

–07' Mars appears to have moved backwards 7 minutes

After calculating the daily motion of each planet, and noting the retrogrades with an Rx for later reference, you will need another calculation to determine how far each body traveled in 21 hours and 36 minutes. This is done quite simply by decimalizing the birth time and dividing by 24, (24 hours of daily motion):

21:36 GMT

Divide minutes by 60: 36 ÷ 60 = .6

Time expressed as decimal: 21.6

21.6 ÷ 24 = .9 <u>Constant Multiplier</u>

This calculation is an important number. This is the constant that we will use to calculate the interval motion of the planets which you have just determined. With these totals in hand, proceed to multiply each planet's daily motion by the constant:

– 07'   ♂ Rx Daily Motion

<u>x.9 = </u>   Constant

   6.3 is the total, but because .3 only equals 18 seconds it is too small a number to have any affect our calculations, and is discarded.

–6 is the total distance traveled by Mars in 21 hours and 36 minutes.

You will be working with mixed quantities in these calculations, as well as clock times. Each column of numbers: 'Hours:Minutes:Seconds' must be calculated individually, beginning with the furthest column to the right, the seconds column. To simplify calculation round up any seconds columns that are 30 and above to whole minutes, and if the seconds are less than 30, just drop them, as they will be inconsequential here. Do not round up the degrees/hours of any planet, Example:

☉ 27 36 08 Becomes:

   27 36

Now back to our Sun calculations:

☉   27:36   July 21

   <u>–26:39 =</u> July 20

       57'

We have a total of 57 minutes of daily motion for the Sun. Multiply the daily motion by the constant:

   57'   Daily motion of Sun

x.9 = Constant

51   Interval

The next step is to add the interval to the GMT time of the Sun on the birth date:

☉   26 39 July 20

+   51 =

26 90   Raw data

☉   27°♋30' Final EGMT Position of Sun

As you work you will, no doubt, run into numbers that exceed '60' in the minutes and seconds columns, and that exceed '30' in the hours columns. Record each set of numbers in the proper column as raw data, and make adjustments later. Now onto the Moon:

☾   11 ♋ 01   July 21

−27 ♊ 48 =   July 20

Before we can go further with this calculation there is something else we must do. On midnight of the day our Female Child was born, the Moon was at 27 ♊ 48, and by the following midnight was at 11 ♋ 01. In order to subtract 27 degrees of Gemini from 11 degrees of Cancer we have to make another adjustment. Since Cancer is the next sign, and is 30 degrees father along in the zodiac, we have to add those 30 degrees to the degrees of the Moon to give us a number that we can work with:

☾   41 01   July 21

☾ − 27 48 = July 20

13 13

The Moon traveled 13 degrees 13 minutes in 24 hours. This calculation will take a bit more work than the others because of the distance that the Moon travels in a 24 hour period. We have 13°13' of daily motion, and we have to convert this data into a decimal in order to multiply by the constant. But first we have to convert all the degrees and minutes into *minutes only* for simplification:

13 degrees x 60 minutes = 780

Plus 13 leftover minutes = 793

793 x .9 = 713.7 – Rounded up to 714

714 ÷ 60 = 11.9

Now we have 11 degrees and .9 leftover; multiply .9 by 60 to turn this decimal back into minutes: .9 x 60 = 54

The Moon's interval in 21 hours, 36 minutes was 11°54'. Now we add this interval to the Moon's position on July 20:

☾   27°♊48'   July 20

+ 11° 54' =   Moon's Interval

   38 102   Raw Data   *The next step should look like this:*

38¹ 102

___- 60 =___

39° 42'

–30 =

☾ 9° ♋ 42   EGMT Position

38 degrees became 39 because we carried over that minute into the degrees column. Then we had too many degrees, so we subtracted the 30 degrees that we had to borrow earlier. This gave us the final position of the Moon on July 20, 1971 at 21:36 hours. Since the Moon travels so much faster, this calculation has more necessary steps. Each step along the way should make rational sense to the student – **at each step know what you are doing and why**. (You will find that each planet has a range of daily motion depending on the time of year, and in time this will become second nature to you. The Moon can travel up to 14° in 24 hours.)

Now onto Mercury:

☿   23 04   July 21
  − 21 44 = July 20
      1° 20'   Add degrees and minutes together to get:
      80   1 degree and 20 minutes = 80 minutes
    80 x .9 = 72   Interval in 21:36 hours
    72 − 60 = 1° 12'   Adjusted back into degrees and
                          minutes
☿   21 44   July 20
  + 1 12 =
    22° ♌ 56' Final EGMT Position of Mercury

Venus:

♀   17 ♋ 14   July 21
  − 16 ♋ 01 = July 20
      1° 13'   (73')
       73 x .9 = 65.7 Multiply by constant, round up
                          to 66
       66 = 1° 06' Adjust back into degrees and minutes
♀   16° ♋ 01'   July 20
  + 1   06 =
    17° ♋ 07' Final EGMT Position of Venus

After calculating the daily motion for each planet, then multiplying each sum by the constant, ADD the interval to the position of each planet on the **date of the birth** at midnight. In the case of retrogrades SUBTRACT the interval from the position of the planet at midnight on the birth date. Remember – the Sun and Moon never retrograde. Record each EGMT position with the proper zodiac sign and retrograde if applicable. Earlier we began the calculations for Mars retrograde, (Rx). We found that Mars appeared to have moved backwards by about 6 minutes. Mars' position on July 20 was 21° ♒ 28' Rx.

♂   21° ♒ 28'   July 20

−   06 =

♂   21° ♒ 22' Rx   Final EGMT Position of Mars

Finish calculating the planetary positions, record them, and we will go onto house calculations.

CALCULATING THE HOUSE CUSPS

House cusp calculation requires more time adjustments. The next adjustment is to the interval after 12:00 midnight that the birth occurred. Using the same example as before, we have now determined that the birth occurred at 21:36:00 hours, Greenwich time, on July 20, 1971. In order to determine the house cusps we have to make some additional calculations with our sidereal time (ST) for July 20. Our PM time is 21 hours 36 minutes. The next step is to add the adjusted birth time to the sidereal time for July 20, 1971.

On the ephemeris page for July 1971, the first column to the left of the Sun is labeled **Sidereal Time**. *Be careful not to confuse this column with the column for the Sun, this is a very common mistake.* Sidereal time is expressed always in hours, minutes and seconds, goes up to 23:59:59, and returns to 00:00:00. **We never – ever round sidereal time up or down**. Use this time exactly as you find it in the ephemeris.

6) 19:48:30   ST July 20, 1971

7) +21:36:00 =   Interval

8) 40:84:30   Corrected ST (Unadjusted)

As you can see, there is more adjusting to be done. In the second column there are 84 minutes, and since we cannot have more than 59 minutes and 59 seconds, (60), you will have to subtract 60, leaving a total of 24 minutes in the middle column.

Carry that 60 minutes, (1 hour of sidereal time) over to the first column to give a total of 41 hours. That give us 40 hours of sidereal time! Since sidereal time only goes up to 23:59:59 and then begins again at 00:00:00, you must subtract 24 hours, giving a total of 17 hours in the first column.

40:84:30 Adjusted = 41:24:30

41:24:30

<u>–24 hrs =</u>

8) 17:24:30 — Corrected ST

Since we are dealing in Sidereal Time, a third adjustment is necessary to obtain the correct Greenwich Mean Time (GMT), or Greenwich Sidereal Time at hour of birth. This adjustment is called "solar-sidereal time correction", and alternatively "acceleration on the interval". (Tables 6A & 6B) This correction is considered in minutes and seconds. The interval, as we have determined, is the period after midnight that the birth occurred. In our example, the interval is +21 hours 36 minutes. Above is a reprinted Solar-Sidereal correction chart. Determine the Interval by locating the native's birth time, 21h, across the top row of the solar–sidereal time correction chart, then follow that column down until you get to the minutes of the native's birth time, 36. You should have ended up with 3 minutes, 33 seconds.

To continue our example:

17:24:30 — Corrected ST

<u>+03:33 =</u> — Acceleration

17:27:63 — Raw Data

18) 17:28:03 — Corrected GMT

Now that we have determined the correct sidereal time of birth at Greenwich we can move on to the next step. One final adjustment is necessary. The longitude and latitude of the place of birth must be determined to calculate a precise horoscope, or natal chart. We have, up to this point, been working with

MIN	0h m	0h s	1h m	1h s	2h m	2h s	3h m	3h s	4h m	4h s	5h m	5h s	6h m	6h s	7h m	7h s	8h m	8h s	9h m	9h s	10h m	10h s	11h m	11h s
0	0	0	0	10	0	20	0	30	0	39	0	49	0	59	1	9	1	19	1	29	1	39	1	48
1	0	0	0	10	0	20	0	30	0	40	0	49	0	59	1	9	1	19	1	29	1	39	1	49
2	0	0	0	10	0	20	0	30	0	40	0	50	0	59	1	9	1	19	1	29	1	39	1	49
3	0	0	0	10	0	20	0	30	0	40	0	50	0	60	1	9	1	19	1	29	1	39	1	49
4	0	1	0	11	0	20	0	30	0	40	0	50	0	60	1	10	1	20	1	29	1	39	1	49
5	0	1	0	11	0	21	0	30	0	40	0	50	0	60	1	10	1	20	1	30	1	39	1	49
6	0	1	0	11	0	21	0	31	0	40	0	50	1	0	1	10	1	20	1	30	1	40	1	49
7	0	1	0	11	0	21	0	31	0	41	0	50	1	0	1	10	1	20	1	30	1	40	1	50
8	0	1	0	11	0	21	0	31	0	41	0	51	1	0	1	10	1	20	1	30	1	40	1	50
9	0	1	0	11	0	21	0	31	0	41	0	51	1	1	1	10	1	20	1	30	1	40	1	50
10	0	2	0	11	0	21	0	31	0	41	0	51	1	1	1	11	1	20	1	30	1	40	1	50
11	0	2	0	12	0	22	0	31	0	41	0	51	1	1	1	11	1	21	1	31	1	40	1	50
12	0	2	0	12	0	22	0	32	0	41	0	51	1	1	1	11	1	21	1	31	1	41	1	50
13	0	2	0	12	0	22	0	32	0	42	0	51	1	1	1	11	1	21	1	31	1	41	1	51
14	0	2	0	12	0	22	0	32	0	42	0	52	1	1	1	11	1	21	1	31	1	41	1	51
15	0	2	0	12	0	22	0	32	0	42	0	52	1	2	1	11	1	21	1	31	1	41	1	51
16	0	3	0	12	0	22	0	32	0	42	0	52	1	2	1	12	1	21	1	31	1	41	1	51
17	0	3	0	13	0	23	0	32	0	42	0	52	1	2	1	12	1	22	1	32	1	41	1	51
18	0	3	0	13	0	23	0	33	0	42	0	52	1	2	1	12	1	22	1	32	1	42	1	51
19	0	3	0	13	0	23	0	33	0	43	0	52	1	2	1	12	1	22	1	32	1	42	1	52
20	0	3	0	13	0	23	0	33	0	43	0	53	1	2	1	12	1	22	1	32	1	42	1	52
21	0	3	0	13	0	23	0	33	0	43	0	53	1	3	1	12	1	22	1	32	1	42	1	52
22	0	4	0	13	0	23	0	33	0	43	0	53	1	3	1	13	1	22	1	32	1	42	1	52
23	0	4	0	14	0	23	0	33	0	43	0	53	1	3	1	13	1	23	1	32	1	42	1	52
24	0	4	0	14	0	24	0	34	0	43	0	53	1	3	1	13	1	23	1	33	1	43	1	52
25	0	4	0	14	0	24	0	34	0	44	0	53	1	3	1	13	1	23	1	33	1	43	1	53
26	0	4	0	14	0	24	0	34	0	44	0	54	1	3	1	13	1	23	1	33	1	43	1	53
27	0	4	0	14	0	24	0	34	0	44	0	54	1	4	1	13	1	23	1	33	1	43	1	53
28	0	5	0	14	0	24	0	34	0	44	0	54	1	4	1	14	1	23	1	33	1	43	1	53
29	0	5	0	15	0	24	0	34	0	44	0	54	1	4	1	14	1	24	1	33	1	43	1	53
30	0	5	0	15	0	25	0	34	0	44	0	54	1	4	1	14	1	24	1	34	1	43	1	53
31	0	5	0	15	0	25	0	35	0	45	0	54	1	4	1	14	1	24	1	34	1	44	1	54
32	0	5	0	15	0	25	0	35	0	45	0	55	1	4	1	14	1	24	1	34	1	44	1	54
33	0	5	0	15	0	25	0	35	0	45	0	55	1	5	1	14	1	24	1	34	1	44	1	54
34	0	6	0	15	0	25	0	35	0	45	0	55	1	5	1	15	1	24	1	34	1	44	1	54
35	0	6	0	16	0	25	0	35	0	45	0	55	1	5	1	15	1	25	1	34	1	44	1	54
36	0	6	0	16	0	26	0	35	0	45	0	55	1	5	1	15	1	25	1	35	1	44	1	54
37	0	6	0	16	0	26	0	36	0	46	0	55	1	5	1	15	1	25	1	35	1	45	1	54
38	0	6	0	16	0	26	0	36	0	46	0	56	1	5	1	15	1	25	1	35	1	45	1	55
39	0	6	0	16	0	26	0	36	0	46	0	56	1	6	1	15	1	25	1	35	1	45	1	55
40	0	7	0	16	0	26	0	36	0	46	0	56	1	6	1	16	1	25	1	35	1	45	1	55
41	0	7	0	17	0	26	0	36	0	46	0	56	1	6	1	16	1	26	1	35	1	45	1	55
42	0	7	0	17	0	27	0	36	0	46	0	56	1	6	1	16	1	26	1	36	1	45	1	55
43	0	7	0	17	0	27	0	37	0	46	0	56	1	6	1	16	1	26	1	36	1	46	1	55
44	0	7	0	17	0	27	0	37	0	47	0	57	1	6	1	16	1	26	1	36	1	46	1	56
45	0	7	0	17	0	27	0	37	0	47	0	57	1	7	1	16	1	26	1	36	1	46	1	56
46	0	8	0	17	0	27	0	37	0	47	0	57	1	7	1	17	1	26	1	36	1	46	1	56
47	0	8	0	18	0	27	0	37	0	47	0	57	1	7	1	17	1	27	1	36	1	46	1	56
48	0	8	0	18	0	28	0	37	0	47	0	57	1	7	1	17	1	27	1	37	1	46	1	56
49	0	8	0	18	0	28	0	38	0	47	0	57	1	7	1	17	1	27	1	37	1	47	1	56
50	0	8	0	18	0	28	0	38	0	48	0	57	1	7	1	17	1	27	1	37	1	47	1	57
51	0	8	0	18	0	28	0	38	0	48	0	58	1	8	1	17	1	27	1	37	1	47	1	57
52	0	9	0	18	0	28	0	38	0	48	0	58	1	8	1	18	1	27	1	37	1	47	1	57
53	0	9	0	19	0	28	0	38	0	48	0	58	1	8	1	18	1	28	1	37	1	47	1	57
54	0	9	0	19	0	29	0	38	0	48	0	58	1	8	1	18	1	28	1	38	1	47	1	57
55	0	9	0	19	0	29	0	39	0	48	0	58	1	8	1	18	1	28	1	38	1	48	1	57
56	0	9	0	19	0	29	0	39	0	49	0	58	1	8	1	18	1	28	1	38	1	48	1	58
57	0	9	0	19	0	29	0	39	0	49	0	59	1	9	1	18	1	28	1	38	1	48	1	58
58	0	10	0	19	0	29	0	39	0	49	0	59	1	9	1	19	1	28	1	38	1	48	1	58
59	0	10	0	20	0	29	0	39	0	49	0	59	1	9	1	19	1	29	1	38	1	48	1	58
60	0	10	0	20	0	30	0	39	0	49	0	59	1	9	1	19	1	29	1	39	1	48	1	58

Table 6-A. Solar-Sidereal Time Correction Table, 0 hours through 11:59 hours. (Alternatively known as acceleration on the interval)

12h		13h		14h		15h		16h		17h		18h		19h		20h		21h		22h		23h		MIN
m	s	m	s	m	s	m	s	m	s	m	s	m	s	m	s	m	s	m	s	m	s	m	s	
1	58	2	8	2	18	2	28	2	38	2	48	2	57	3	7	3	17	3	27	3	37	3	47	0
1	58	2	8	2	18	2	28	2	38	2	48	2	58	3	7	3	17	3	27	3	37	3	47	1
1	59	2	8	2	18	2	28	2	38	2	48	2	58	3	8	3	17	3	27	3	37	3	47	2
1	59	2	9	2	18	2	28	2	38	2	48	2	58	3	8	3	18	3	27	3	37	3	47	3
1	59	2	9	2	19	2	29	2	38	2	48	2	58	3	8	3	18	3	28	3	37	3	47	4
1	59	2	9	2	19	2	29	2	39	2	48	2	58	3	8	3	18	3	28	3	38	3	48	5
1	59	2	9	2	19	2	29	2	39	2	49	2	58	3	8	3	18	3	28	3	38	3	48	6
1	59	2	9	2	19	2	29	2	39	2	49	2	59	3	8	3	18	3	28	3	38	3	48	7
1	60	2	9	2	19	2	29	2	39	2	49	2	59	3	9	3	18	3	28	3	38	3	48	8
1	60	2	10	2	19	2	29	2	39	2	49	2	59	3	9	3	19	3	28	3	38	3	48	9
1	60	2	10	2	20	2	29	2	39	2	49	2	59	3	9	3	19	3	29	3	38	3	48	10
2	0	2	10	2	20	2	30	2	40	2	49	2	59	3	9	3	19	3	29	3	39	3	49	11
2	0	2	10	2	20	2	30	2	40	2	50	2	59	3	9	3	19	3	29	3	39	3	49	12
2	0	2	10	2	20	2	30	2	40	2	50	2	60	3	9	3	19	3	29	3	39	3	49	13
2	1	2	10	2	20	2	30	2	40	2	50	2	60	3	10	3	19	3	29	3	39	3	49	14
2	1	2	11	2	20	2	30	2	40	2	50	2	60	3	10	3	20	3	29	3	39	3	49	15
2	1	2	11	2	21	2	30	2	40	2	50	3	0	3	10	3	20	3	30	3	39	3	49	16
2	1	2	11	2	21	2	31	2	40	2	50	3	0	3	10	3	20	3	30	3	40	3	49	17
2	1	2	11	2	21	2	31	2	41	2	51	3	0	3	10	3	20	3	30	3	40	3	50	18
2	1	2	11	2	21	2	31	2	41	2	51	3	1	3	10	3	20	3	30	3	40	3	50	19
2	2	2	11	2	21	2	31	2	41	2	51	3	1	3	11	3	20	3	30	3	40	3	50	20
2	2	2	12	2	21	2	31	2	41	2	51	3	1	3	11	3	21	3	30	3	40	3	50	21
2	2	2	12	2	22	2	31	2	41	2	51	3	1	3	11	3	21	3	31	3	40	3	50	22
2	2	2	12	2	22	2	32	2	41	2	51	3	1	3	11	3	21	3	31	3	41	3	50	23
2	2	2	12	2	22	2	32	2	42	2	52	3	1	3	11	3	21	3	31	3	41	3	51	24
2	2	2	12	2	22	2	32	2	42	2	52	3	2	3	11	3	21	3	31	3	41	3	51	25
2	3	2	12	2	22	2	32	2	42	2	52	3	2	3	12	3	21	3	31	3	41	3	51	26
2	3	2	13	2	22	2	32	2	42	2	52	3	2	3	12	3	22	3	31	3	41	3	51	27
2	3	2	13	2	23	2	32	2	42	2	52	3	2	3	12	3	22	3	32	3	41	3	51	28
2	3	2	13	2	23	2	33	2	42	2	52	3	2	3	12	3	22	3	32	3	42	3	51	29
2	3	2	13	2	23	2	33	2	43	2	52	3	2	3	12	3	22	3	32	3	42	3	52	30
2	3	2	13	2	23	2	33	2	43	2	53	3	3	3	12	3	22	3	32	3	42	3	52	31
2	4	2	13	2	23	2	33	2	43	2	53	3	3	3	13	3	22	3	32	3	42	3	52	32
2	4	2	14	2	23	2	33	2	43	2	53	3	3	3	13	3	23	3	32	3	42	3	52	33
2	4	2	14	2	24	2	33	2	43	2	53	3	3	3	13	3	23	3	33	3	42	3	52	34
2	4	2	14	2	24	2	34	2	43	2	53	3	3	3	13	3	23	3	33	3	43	3	52	35
2	4	2	14	2	24	2	34	2	44	2	53	3	3	3	13	3	23	3	33	3	43	3	53	36
2	4	2	14	2	24	2	34	2	44	2	54	3	3	3	13	3	23	3	33	3	43	3	53	37
2	5	2	14	2	24	2	34	2	44	2	54	3	4	3	14	3	23	3	33	3	43	3	53	38
2	5	2	15	2	24	2	34	2	44	2	54	3	4	3	14	3	24	3	33	3	43	3	53	39
2	5	2	15	2	25	2	34	2	44	2	54	3	4	3	14	3	24	3	34	3	43	3	53	40
2	5	2	15	2	25	2	35	2	44	2	54	3	4	3	14	3	24	3	34	3	44	3	53	41
2	5	2	15	2	25	2	35	2	45	2	54	3	4	3	14	3	24	3	34	3	44	3	54	42
2	5	2	15	2	25	2	35	2	45	2	55	3	4	3	14	3	24	3	34	3	44	3	54	43
2	6	2	15	2	25	2	35	2	45	2	55	3	5	3	15	3	24	3	34	3	44	3	54	44
2	6	2	16	2	25	2	35	2	45	2	55	3	5	3	15	3	25	3	34	3	44	3	54	45
2	6	2	16	2	26	2	35	2	45	2	55	3	5	3	15	3	25	3	35	3	44	3	54	46
2	6	2	16	2	26	2	36	2	45	2	55	3	5	3	15	3	25	3	35	3	45	3	54	47
2	6	2	16	2	26	2	36	2	46	2	55	3	5	3	15	3	25	3	35	3	45	3	55	48
2	6	2	16	2	26	2	36	2	46	2	56	3	5	3	15	3	25	3	35	3	45	3	55	49
2	6	2	16	2	26	2	36	2	46	2	56	3	6	3	15	3	25	3	35	3	45	3	55	50
2	7	2	17	2	26	2	36	2	46	2	56	3	6	3	16	3	26	3	35	3	45	3	55	51
2	7	2	17	2	27	2	36	2	46	2	56	3	6	3	16	3	26	3	36	3	45	3	55	52
2	7	2	17	2	27	2	37	2	46	2	56	3	6	3	16	3	26	3	36	3	46	3	55	53
2	7	2	17	2	27	2	37	2	47	2	56	3	6	3	16	3	26	3	36	3	46	3	55	54
2	7	2	17	2	27	2	37	2	47	2	57	3	6	3	16	3	26	3	36	3	46	3	56	55
2	7	2	17	2	27	2	37	2	47	2	57	3	7	3	16	3	26	3	36	3	46	3	56	56
2	8	2	17	2	27	2	37	2	47	2	57	3	7	3	17	3	26	3	36	3	46	3	56	57
2	8	2	18	2	28	2	37	2	47	2	57	3	7	3	17	3	27	3	37	3	46	3	56	58
2	8	2	18	2	28	2	38	2	47	2	57	3	7	3	17	3	27	3	37	3	47	3	56	59
2	8	2	18	2	28	2	38	2	48	2	57	3	7	3	17	3	27	3	37	3	47	3	57	60

Table 6-B. Solar-Sidereal Time Correction Table, 12 hours through 23:59 hours. (Alternatively known as acceleration on the interval)

planetary positions from Greenwich, and now we have to place this information in a specific location: the native's place of birth. A Latitude and Longitude Table, or Atlas will be most useful to determine the latitude and longitude for the place of birth if one is not provided. (Also, make use of internet resources, it is easy these days to obtain the coordinates of a city or town with an online check.) Lets continue with our Female Child's natal chart calculations.

Salt Lake City, Utah is located at latitude 40° N 45' 39", longitude 111° W 53' 25". Lets round up those seconds and simplify the calculation: lat: 40° N 46', long: 111° W 53'. Our GMT is 17:28:06. But what we need to know right now is what was the sidereal time where the Female Child was born? We call this Local Sidereal Time. To get Local Sidereal Time (LST), we must convert the longitude to time. The formula for this conversion is:

Longitude x 4 ÷ 60 = time

1) Multiply the degrees of longitude by 4; convert to hours and minutes

2) Divide minutes of longitude by 60 to obtain decimal number, round up to 2 digits

3) Multiply decimal number by 4, convert to minutes and seconds

Lets try that with Female Child's longitude 111° W 53':

111° West longitude x 4= 444

444 ÷ 60 = 7.4 (Seven hours and .4 minutes leftover)

.4 x 60 = 24 (Convert decimal to minutes, now we have 7:24)

53 ÷ 60 = .88 (Minutes column of longitude decimalized)

.88 x 4 = **3**.52 (Decimalized minutes multiplied by 4)

.52 x 60 = **31** (Convert decimal to seconds)

10ʰ 0ᵐ 0ˢ		MC	150° 0' 0"		N
		♌ 27° 49' 5"			LAT
11	12	Ascendant	2	3	
♎ 0° 0.0'	♏ 2° 10.9'	♐ 2° 5.4'	♑ 0° 0.0'	♒ 27° 54.6'	0°
0 0.0	1 26.6	0 19.3	♐28 40.2	27 18.4	5
0 0.0	0 43.4	♏28 35.3	27 19.3	26 41.3	10
0 0.0	0 0.7	26 51.8	25 55.8	26 2.4	15
0 0.0	♎29 52.1	26 31.1	25 38.7	25 54.4	16
0 0.0	29 43.6	26 10.3	25 21.4	25 46.2	17
0 0.0	29 35.0	25 49.5	25 3.9	25 38.0	18
0 0.0	29 26.4	25 28.6	24 46.3	25 29.6	19
0 0.0	29 17.8	25 7.7	24 28.4	25 21.1	20
0 0.0	29 9.1	24 46.6	24 10.3	25 12.4	21
0 0.0	29 0.4	24 25.4	23 52.0	25 3.7	22
0 0.0	28 51.7	24 4.2	23 33.4	24 54.7	23
0 0.0	28 42.9	23 42.8	23 14.6	24 45.6	24
0 0.0	28 34.0	23 21.3	22 55.4	24 36.3	25
0 0.0	28 25.1	22 59.6	22 36.0	24 26.8	26
0 0.0	28 16.1	22 37.7	22 16.2	24 17.1	27
0 0.0	28 7.1	22 15.7	21 56.0	24 7.2	28
0 0.0	27 58.0	21 53.5	21 35.6	23 57.1	29
0 0.0	27 48.7	21 31.1	21 14.7	23 46.7	30
0 0.0	27 39.4	21 8.5	20 53.4	23 36.1	31
0 0.0	27 30.0	20 45.6	20 31.6	23 25.2	32
0 0.0	27 20.5	20 22.5	20 9.4	23 13.9	33
0 0.0	27 10.9	19 59.1	19 46.7	23 2.4	34
0 0.0	27 1.1	19 35.4	19 23.5	22 50.5	35
0 0.0	26 51.2	19 11.5	18 59.7	22 38.3	36
0 0.0	26 41.2	18 47.2	18 35.4	22 25.6	37
0 0.0	26 31.0	18 22.5	18 10.4	22 12.6	38
0 0.0	26 20.6	17 57.6	17 44.7	21 59.1	39
0 0.0	26 10.1	17 32.2	17 18.3	21 45.1	40
0 0.0	25 59.4	17 6.4	16 51.2	21 30.5	41
0 0.0	25 48.5	16 40.2	16 23.2	21 15.4	42
0 0.0	25 37.4	16 13.6	15 54.4	20 59.7	43
0 0.0	25 26.1	15 46.5	15 24.7	20 43.3	44
0 0.0	25 14.6	15 18.9	14 54.0	20 26.2	45
0 0.0	25 2.8	14 50.8	14 22.3	20 8.3	46
0 0.0	24 50.7	14 22.1	13 49.4	19 49.5	47
0 0.0	24 38.4	13 52.8	13 15.4	19 29.7	48
0 0.0	24 25.8	13 22.9	12 40.0	19 8.9	49
0 0.0	24 12.9	12 52.4	12 3.3	18 47.0	50
0 0.0	23 59.6	12 21.1	11 25.2	18 23.7	51
0 0.0	23 46.1	11 49.2	10 45.4	17 59.0	52
0 0.0	23 32.1	11 16.5	10 3.9	17 32.7	53
0 0.0	23 17.7	10 42.9	9 20.6	17 4.5	54
0 0.0	23 2.9	10 8.6	8 35.4	16 34.3	55
0 0.0	22 47.7	9 33.3	7 47.9	16 1.6	56
0 0.0	22 32.0	8 57.0	6 58.2	15 26.2	57
0 0.0	22 15.8	8 19.8	6 6.0	14 47.6	58
0 0.0	21 59.0	7 41.5	5 11.0	14 5.1	59
0 0.0	21 41.6	7 2.1	4 13.1	13 17.9	60
0 0.0	21 23.7	6 21.5	3 11.9	12 24.9	61
0 0.0	21 5.0	5 39.7	2 7.3	11 24.3	62
0 0.0	20 45.7	4 56.5	0 58.8	10 13.7	63
0 0.0	20 25.5	4 11.9	♏29 46.2	8 48.5	64
0 0.0	20 4.6	3 25.8	28 29.0	6 59.1	65
0 0.0	19 42.7	2 38.2	27 6.9	4 15.0	66
5	6	Descendant	8	9	S
		♒ 27° 49' 5"			LAT
22ʰ 0ᵐ 0ˢ		MC	330° 0' 0"		

Table 7-A. Table of Placidus Houses
10h0m0s

	10ʰ 4ᵐ 0ˢ		MC	151° 0′ 0″	
N LAT	11	12	Ascendant ♌ 28° 51′ 38″	2	3
0	♎ 1 5.4	♏ 3 13.3	♐ 3 2.6	♑ 0 55.0	♑ 28 52.0
5	1 4.6	2 27.7	1 15.7	♐ 29 35.3	28 16.1
10	1 3.8	1 43.3	♏ 29 30.7	28 14.2	27 39.2
15	1 3.0	0 59.4	27 46.3	26 50.6	27 0.6
16	1 2.8	0 50.6	27 25.3	26 33.4	26 52.6
17	1 2.6	0 41.8	27 4.3	26 16.1	26 44.5
18	1 2.5	0 33.0	26 43.3	25 58.6	26 36.3
19	1 2.3	0 24.1	26 22.1	25 40.9	26 28.0
20	1 2.1	0 15.3	26 0.9	25 23.0	26 19.6
21	1 2.0	0 6.3	25 39.6	25 4.8	26 11.0
22	1 1.8	♎ 29 57.4	25 18.2	24 46.4	26 2.2
23	1 1.6	29 48.4	24 56.7	24 27.8	25 53.3
24	1 1.4	29 39.3	24 35.1	24 8.9	25 44.3
25	1 1.3	29 30.2	24 13.3	23 49.7	25 35.0
26	1 1.1	29 21.0	23 51.3	23 30.1	25 25.6
27	1 0.9	29 11.8	23 29.2	23 10.3	25 16.0
28	1 0.7	29 2.5	23 6.9	22 50.0	25 6.1
29	1 0.5	28 53.1	22 44.4	22 29.5	24 56.1
30	1 0.4	28 43.6	22 21.7	22 8.5	24 45.7
31	1 0.2	28 34.0	21 58.8	21 47.1	24 35.2
32	1 0.0	28 24.3	21 35.6	21 25.2	24 24.3
33	0 59.8	28 14.5	21 12.2	21 2.9	24 13.1
34	0 59.6	28 4.5	20 48.4	20 40.1	24 1.7
35	0 59.4	27 54.4	20 24.4	20 16.7	23 49.8
36	0 59.2	27 44.2	20 0.1	19 52.8	23 37.7
37	0 59.0	27 33.9	19 35.5	19 28.3	23 25.1
38	0 58.8	27 23.4	19 10.5	19 3.1	23 12.1
39	0 58.5	27 12.7	18 45.2	18 37.3	22 58.6
40	0 58.3	27 1.9	18 19.4	18 10.7	22 44.7
41	0 58.1	26 50.8	17 53.3	17 43.3	22 30.2
42	0 57.9	26 39.6	17 26.7	17 15.2	22 15.2
43	0 57.6	26 28.2	16 59.6	16 46.2	21 59.6
44	0 57.4	26 16.5	16 32.1	16 16.2	21 43.2
45	0 57.1	26 4.6	16 4.0	15 45.2	21 26.2
46	0 56.9	25 52.4	15 35.5	15 13.2	21 8.3
47	0 56.6	25 40.0	15 6.3	14 40.1	20 49.6
48	0 56.4	25 27.3	14 36.6	14 5.7	20 30.0
49	0 56.1	25 14.3	14 6.2	13 30.0	20 9.2
50	0 55.8	25 0.9	13 35.1	12 52.9	19 47.4
51	0 55.5	24 47.2	13 3.4	12 14.4	19 24.2
52	0 55.2	24 33.2	12 30.9	11 34.2	18 59.6
53	0 54.9	24 18.7	11 57.6	10 52.2	18 33.3
54	0 54.5	24 3.9	11 23.5	10 8.4	18 5.3
55	0 54.2	23 48.7	10 48.5	9 22.6	17 35.1
56	0 53.9	23 32.9	10 12.6	8 34.5	17 2.6
57	0 53.5	23 16.7	9 35.7	7 44.1	16 27.3
58	0 53.1	22 59.9	8 57.8	6 51.2	15 48.8
59	0 52.7	22 42.6	8 18.9	5 55.4	15 6.4
60	0 52.3	22 24.7	7 38.7	4 56.6	14 19.3
61	0 51.9	22 6.1	6 57.4	3 54.5	13 26.4
62	0 51.4	21 46.8	6 14.8	2 48.8	12 26.0
63	0 50.9	21 26.8	5 30.8	1 39.1	11 15.6
64	0 50.4	21 6.0	4 45.4	0 25.2	9 50.5
65	0 49.9	20 44.3	3 58.4	♏ 29 6.6	8 1.4
66	0 49.4	20 21.7	3 9.9	27 42.8	5 17.5
S LAT	5	6	Descendant ♒ 28° 51′ 38″	8	9
	22ʰ 4ᵐ 0ˢ		MC	331° 0′ 0″	

Table 7-B. Table of Placidus Houses
10h4m0s

7h 24m 00s

+   03m 31s =

7:27:31

The longitude in our example is West, and so we subtract it from the GMT. (If the longitude had been East, we would have added it to the GMT. As mentioned earlier, we will address eastern locations in Chapter 6.)

17:28:03 — GMT

-7:27:31 = — Salt Lake City Longitude Time

10:00:32 — Local Sidereal Time, or LST

This was the final step in adjusting the birth time. We can now proceed to erect the natal chart, using our Ephemeris and Table of Houses.

*One rule which we have not discussed: Whenever any step in this procedure cannot be completed due to subtraction that goes into negative numbers, or addition that goes beyond 24 hours, 24 hours may be added or subtracted as necessary. (Similarly, when we calculated the Moon's position, we added and subtracted the 30 degrees of a **sign**.)

Next turn to the tables of houses for the nearest sidereal time to **10h 00m 32s**, at the latitude of Salt Lake City. The following data are copied from Placidus Table of Houses. Sidereal time will be printed in the upper left corner of the table. Note the tables are exactly four minutes apart from each other in time. Our LST of 10:00:06 falls between **10h 0m 0s and 10h 4m 0s**.

Refer to table 7. Each houses table ranges from 0° to 66°. At this point in our calculations we must determine the house cusps to the nearest minute, and for this we need the exact degrees and minutes of the native's birth latitude. Our example person was born between latitudes 40° and 41°.

10h 0m 0s is the LESSER sidereal time, 10h 4m 0s is the GREATER sidereal time, exactly 4 minutes apart. Female

Child's sidereal birth time is 10h 0m 32s. Subtracting the lesser sidereal time from the birth sidereal time, leaves a mere 32 seconds left over. The sum that we get from this calculation is used to get a new constant multiplier, and is done slightly differently.

32 ÷ 60 = .53 (Convert to decimal)

.53 ÷ 4 = .13 (Divide by 4)

Start with the Midheaven, or MC at the greater listed sidereal time, round seconds up, and subtract the lesser MC from the greater MC:

28° ♌ 52'   (MC at 10h04m00s)

-27° ♌ 49 = (MC at 10h00m00s)

   1   03 (One degree plus three minutes = 63 minutes)

63 minutes (63 x .13 = 8)

27° ♌ 49

+   8 =

27° ♌ 57' MC

There are no more calculations for the MC, once you have calculated it, note its sign and degree and move on to the house cusps.

The house cusps are calculated according to the following formula, (remember this is only one of many methods). Read through the instructions and be sure that you understand them. We will go through all the steps afterward when we continue Female Child's horoscope:

1. On Figure 7, the Tables of Houses, note that in between each table of sidereal times is a column of Latitude degrees in bold type. Locate the cusp column beginning with '11' on the table for the GREATER sidereal time; scroll down until you locate the LOWER latitude. Write down the time indicated there. Seconds are normally decimalized on these tables, round

up anything 5 and over, or drop. (Example latitude is 40°N46, so 40° is the LOWER latitude, 41° would be the HIGHER)

2. Next, on the LESSER sidereal table, locate the LOWER latitude in the column for the 11th cusp.
3. Subtract the LESSER sidereal time from the GREATER sidereal time. Multiply the answer by the constant to obtain the interval.
4. Add the interval back to the LESSER listed degrees and minutes. Record answer, go on to the next cusp. (You will be calculating cusps 11, 12, 1, 2, 3, and MC, and from these we derive the rest.)
5. Next, note the degrees and minutes of the GREATER sidereal time at the HIGHER latitude.
6. Note the degrees and minutes of the LESSER sidereal time at the HIGHER latitude.
7. Subtract the LESSER from the GREATER, record answers. Multiply each answer by the constant.
8. Add the new sum back to the LESSER listed degrees and minutes. Record answer, next cusp.
9. After calculating the cusps for the higher and lower latitudes, there will be two sets of sums, one set for the higher latitude and one set for the lower.
10. Take the MINUTES ONLY of the latitude of the native's birth location, and DIVIDE by 60. The answer you get becomes the new constant multiplier.
11. Now, subtract the sums of the LOWER latitude set from the sums of the HIGHER latitude set; multiply by the new constant.
12. Add the answer back to the LESSER listed degrees and minutes. Adjust raw date, put in correct sign.

NOTE: When you get to the third set of calculations, there may very well be sums from the lesser listed times that are greater than the sums for the higher listed times. This is common, so know that it can and does happen, just switch the sums as you would do for retrograde motion and *subtract* normally.

Remember – the constant that we need for the first two sets of calculations is **.13**. We have already calculated the MC, (which is also the 10th house cusp), and the 11th house cusp in this example is practically done for us.

At both lesser sidereal times the 11th cusp is at 0° ♎ 00', and both greater sidereal times the cusps are 0° ♎ 58. We can't subtract 0, so we multiply 58 minutes by the constant, .13 to get: 8 (58 x .13 = 7.54) round up to 8.

We can see that we are going to get 8 for the sum of both listed sidereal times. Following our list of steps, we skip down to step 10 and multiply by the new constant. The third set of calculations is where we need the new constant, which is step 10.

(LATITUDE MINUTES ÷ 60 = constant)

Our latitude is 40° N 46'; (46 ÷ 60 = .77)

(8 x .77 = 6) This is 6 minutes, or 06'

That's it for the 11th house cusp. It is at 0° ♎ 06

12th cusp: At the GREATER listed sidereal time, 40° N latitude, (which is the LOWER latitude), we find 27 ♎ 02.

At the LESSER listed sidereal time, 40° N latitude, we find 26° ♎ 10. Subtract the LESSER from the GREATER to get 52. (52 x .13 = 7) (26 10 + 7 = 26 17)

First calculation: 12th house cusp = 26° 17'

Next: At the GREATER sidereal time, (10:04:00) HIGHER latitude (41°) the 12th cusp is 26 51.

At the LESSER sidereal time (10:00:00) HIGHER latitude

(41°) the 12th cusp is 25° 59'. Simple subtraction gives a sum of 52, which we know from earlier will reduce to 7 after multiplication by the constant. Add the two:

(25 59 + 7 = 25 66) Correct to: 26 06.

Second calculation: 12 house cusp = 26° 06'

Next: Subtract the second set of times from the first set – the lower latitude times from the higher latitude times.

Since we have run into the situation mentioned earlier, in **Your math should look something like the following:**

which our higher latitude numbers are greater than our lower latitude numbers, we treat them the same as we would for retrograde math and end up with a negative number that will be subtracted instead of added.

We end up with –11, which is multiplied by the constant to get: 9. (26 17 – 9 = 26 08) Place in sign: 26 ♎ 08

Ascendant: Asc = First house cusp. At the GREATER listed sidereal time, LOWER latitude find 18° 19'. At the LESSER listed sidereal time find 17° 32'. Simple subtraction gives a total of 47', multiplied by the constant, .13 gives 6. Now add those 6' to 17° 32' to get: <u>17° 38'.</u>

Next: At the GREATER listed sidereal time, LOWER latitude find 17° 53'. At the LESSER listed sidereal time, LOWER latitude find 17° 06'. Subtract for a total of: 47', which multiplied by .13 for a total of 6.

17° 06 + 6 = 17° 12'

Second set total Ascendant = <u>17° 12'</u>

Next: Subtract Set 1 from Set 2, (lower lat from higher lat); multiply sums by constant, add back to the data from the LOWER sidereal time, or subtract as indicated.

~~17° 12~~   17° 38   switch order
~~-17° 38 =~~   -17° 12 =   for calculations
                  –26

26 x .77 = 20   17° 38' – 20 = 17° 18'

Figure 11. Chart wheel with all house cusps filled in.

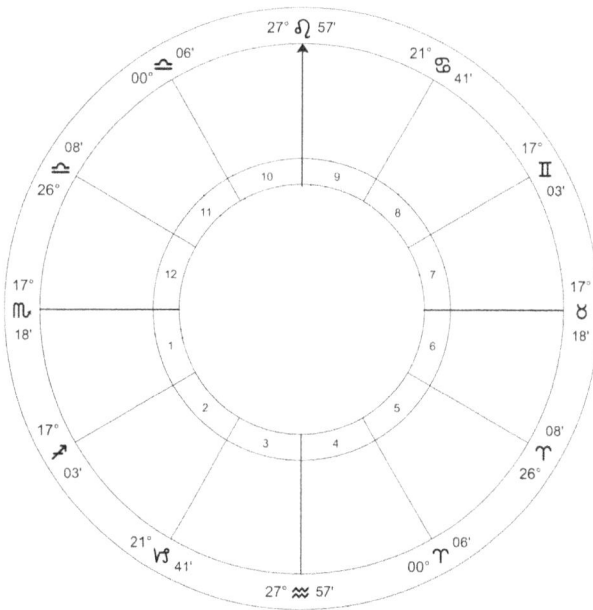

The signs are listed in the columns of the sidereal times; locate the sign at the degree of latitude your cusp is at, and you are finished. The first three cusps are done, and now you can calculate the cusps for houses two and three. This gives you 6 cusps, but we have 12 houses. The other 6 cusps are the exact same times as the first, but are in the opposite signs. The opposite of the 10th house cusp (MC) is the 4th house, so the 4th house cusp should be at 27° ♒ 57'.

Copy this data to the cusps of the houses, and round off to the nearest minute. Fill in the rest of the cusps with the same times as its opposite, change to the corresponding sign. The horoscope will then appear as in Figure 11. The student will note that the zodiacal signs Virgo and Pisces are still missing from the chart and that Libra and Aries each cover two cusps. This is due to the latitude of Salt Lake City, while Earth is tilted

Figure 12. Chart wheel showing intercepted houses

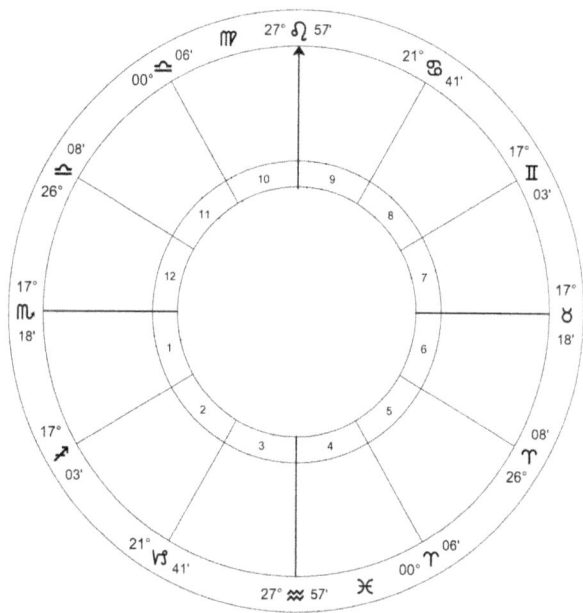

at an angle of 23 degrees and 27 minutes to the ecliptic. The rotation of Earth is therefore at this angle to the ecliptic. (Referring to Chapter 3, it will also be noted that Libra is a sign of long ascension, just longer than the mean rate; and Pisces is short ascension.) They are inserted in their proper sequence, for ALL of the signs of the zodiac always follow in the same order, counterclockwise.

The charts will then appear as in Figure 13 where Virgo and Pisces are termed Intercepted in houses IV and X, (4 & 10)

The next stage is the correct placement of the planets and the luminaries (Sun and Moon) in the horoscope. (Remember, for our purposes we refer to the Sun and Moon as planets, for simplification.)

Note the position of the Sun. At noon the Sun would be on the upper meridian or near the MC, and a few minutes after 11:00 AM the Sun would be approaching the MC. As a spot

Figure 13. Approximate house locations of the Sun by hour of birth

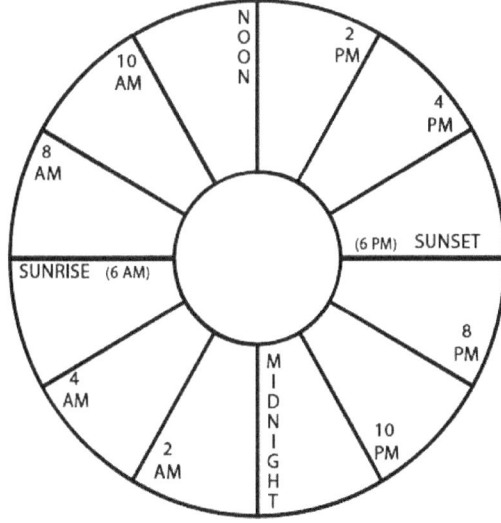

check, use Figure 14 to see if the Sun's position agrees with its physical location in the heavens, remembering that this is simply a map of the ecliptic for the moment of birth. If not, the calculations are in error.

In this horoscope chart the Sun is at 27°♋ 30' and is found in house IX, 30 degrees from the MC. The North Node of the Moon is shown in the ephemeris by degree and sign. Its symbol is written as ☊. The South Node may be placed in the horoscope as well, in the same degree but opposite sign as the N Node, the pair being opposite each other in the chart. These nodes are

Figure 14. Completed natal horoscope chart with planets and N Node.

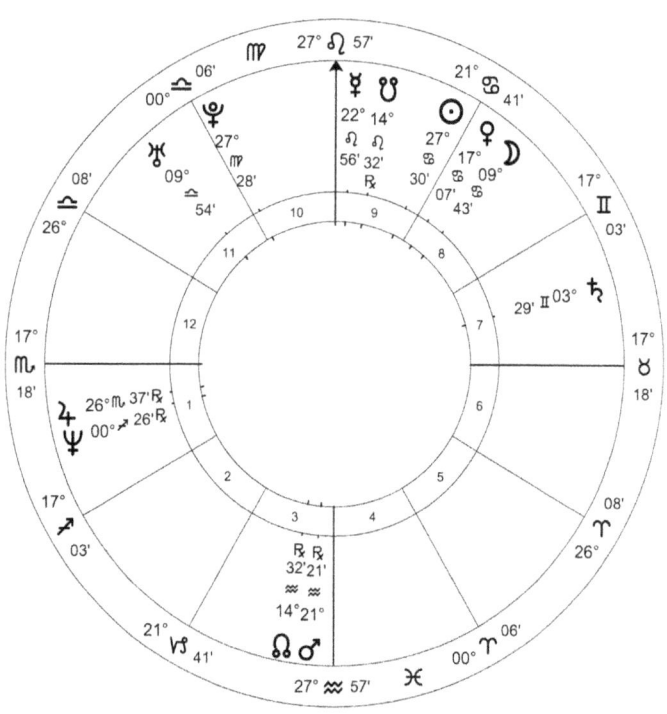

sometimes called the Dragon's Head ☊, and the Dragon's tail, ☋.

Insert all the planets in the chart to complete the birth horoscope, or Nativity, as in Figure 15.

Review Questions For Chapter 5:

1. What basic tools are necessary for erecting a horoscope?

2. List the time zones relevant to the United States and Canada.

3. Calculate the house cusps for the following birth dates and places:

    a) Example A, New York, NY, March 12, 1950, 9:55 AM, EST.

    b) Example B, Santa Monica, CA, February 9, 1945, 11:27 AM, PWT.

4. How is longitude converted into time?

| Chapter 6 |

Other Factors in Creating the Horoscope

THE BASICS NEEDED TO CREATE A horoscope, or natal chart, are the calculation of the house cusps and interpolation of planetary longitudes as discussed in Chapter 5. However, there are other factors to be taken into consideration by the student who seriously contemplates a thorough study of astrology.

DECLINATION

Declinations are found in an ephemeris, although not all ephemerides contain declinations. In an ephemeris, the declinations of the Sun, Moon and planets are given for every day in the month. (In some contemporary ephemerides, declinations are also given for Chiron and the asteroids.) The Declination of a point means its distance, measured in degrees of arc, north or south of the equator. If the declination is north and increasing, the body is moving away from the celestial equator. If the declination is north and decreasing, the body is moving toward the celestial equator. The same is true for planets whose declination is south.

Calculating the precise declination of the Moon, Sun, or any planet is a simple process – the very same process used to calculate planetary longitudes that was covered in Chapter 5. The increase or decrease in declination over 24 hours is calculated, then the constant multiplier for the horoscope, and the resulting interval (reduced to degrees and minutes) is the amount by which the declination must be increased or decreased.

The following example is from Female Child's data in the previous chapter, and as you recall, the constant we found for calculating the planetary longitudes was .9, and we use this same constant for figuring declinations.

Sun Declination

Declination July 21:	20°N 39'
Declination July 20:	-20°N 50'
RESULT: 24–hour motion:	–11'
(11 x .9 = 10)	20°N 50
	– 10
	20°N 40

Declinations can either increase or decrease, so we never know what to expect. In the above example we had another instance of having to change the positions of the numbers so that we could subtract. There will be times when many or all of the declinations are in negative numbers. Don't forget to indicate where you need to subtract the interval rather than add!

Following the procedure we learned to calculate the planetary longitudes for the natal chart, each step along the way is the same. Continue with the Moon and the inner planets as usual. With respect to Jupiter, Saturn, Uranus, Neptune, and Pluto the change is often so negligible that it need not be calculated. For these outer planets the declination given in the ephemeris is often accurate enough.

RETROGRADE MOTION

In Chapter 5, mention has been made of the fact that Mars, Jupiter, and Neptune were retrograde in their apparent motion, i.e., appear to move backward through the zodiac. Actually, they are not moving backward, but Earth's constant revolution around the Sun (in the case of the exterior planets) and the revolution of the interior planets in their orbits cause all of the planets except the Sun and the Moon to appear to move backward from time to time. The cause of this retrograde motion is illustrated in Figures 15 and 16.

SOUTHERN HEMISPHERE BIRTH

The horoscope discussed earlier was for a birth in northern latitudes. But because the astrologer will, no doubt, be expected to create charts for any location in the world, explanation must be made for procedures to calculate births occurring in other parts of the world.

With birth dates south of the equator, the natal chart is prepared differently to account for the changed canopy of the heavens. Local Mean Time would be calculated in the regular manner, as this is based upon longitude, with the Greenwich meridian as the usual starting point. The mathematical calculations based upon the sidereal time given in the ephemeris are also based partially upon longitude, with Zero degree Aries taken as the starting point of the sidereal day in relation to the meridian of Greenwich Mean Time. But, just as the seasons are reversed south of the equator, so these places have an opposite relationship to the zodiac from the northern latitudes. This factor can be accounted for by adding twelve hours to the sidereal time and by

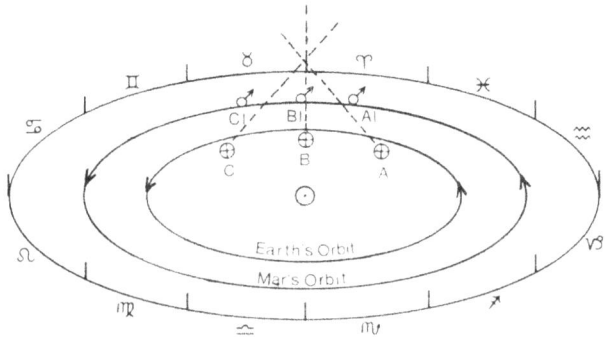

Figure 15. Retrograde motion of an interior, or inferior planet. By apparent motion as seen from Earth, the planet Venus moves from point A to point B, through point D in the diagram above. At point D Venus appears to be moving in a backward motion, or retrograde, as viewed from Earth. Earth is shown in orbit by A1, B1, D1. The Sun is in the center of the diagram surrounded by the zodiacal signs on the outer ring.

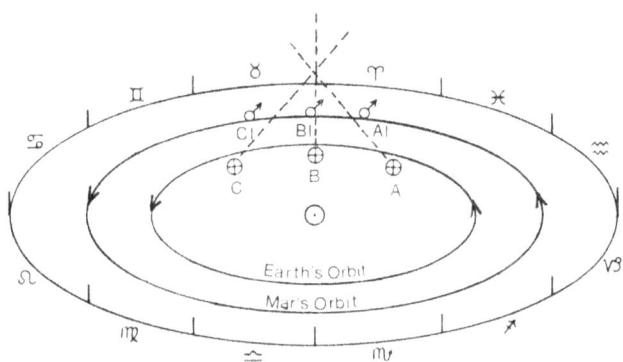

Figure 16. Retrograde motion of an exterior, or superior planet. By apparent motion, as seen from Earth, the planet Mars moves from point A^1 to point C^1, through point B^1, in the diagram above. The Earth would, at the same time be moving through points A, B and C. Between points A^1 and C^1 the movement of Mars would appear to be backwards or retrograde as observed from Earth. The Sun is at the center of the diagram surrounded by the outer circle of zodiacal signs.

also reversing the cusps of the houses. Adding twelve hours accounts for the six month's difference in seasons, since the sidereal day moves forward a full 24 hours in one year, and reversing the house cusps accounts for the reversed appearance of the heavens south of the equator.

Now calculate the natal chart for a birth in the southern hemisphere, yet keeping western longitude. Buenos Aires, Argentina, uses Atlantic Standard Time which is four hours later than Greenwich Mean Time. The suggested birthday is November 23, 1956, at 2:00 PM AST, in Buenos Aires, having a longitude of 58 W 27 and latitude of 34 S 36:

Birth Time:	2:00:00
Add 12 hours for PM birth:	+12:00:00
Difference from GMT to AST:	+ 4:00:00
RESULT Greenwich Mean Time:	18:00:00 GMT
Sidereal time for previous midnight:	4:07:45
Birth time interval from midnight:	18:00:00
Correction for interval:	02:58
Add 12 hours for southern latitude:	+12:00:00
RESULT: Raw Greenwich Sidereal Time:	34:10:43
	−24:00:00
RESULT: Greenwich Sidereal Time:	10:10:43 GST
Longitude Correction (Longitude x 4 ÷ 60 = time):	− 3:53:48
RESULT: Local Sidereal Time:	6:16:55

Now look in the table of houses for the degree of latitude for Buenos Aires. The midheaven becomes the nadir. See below for planetary opposites.

Other Factors in Creating the Horoscope

The planets are calculated in the regular manner at the Greenwich Mean Time of 18:00:00 and then placed in the horoscope in the normal manner. The signs of the planets are not exchanged. (see Figure 17)

ARIES	♈	LIBRA	♎
TAURUS	♉	SCORPIO	♏
GEMINI	♊	SAGITTARIUS	♐
CANCER	♋	CAPRICORN	♑
LEO	♌	AQUARIUS	♒
VIRGO	♍	PISCES	♓

Table of Sign Polarities

Figure 17. Horoscope erected for southern hemisphere example.

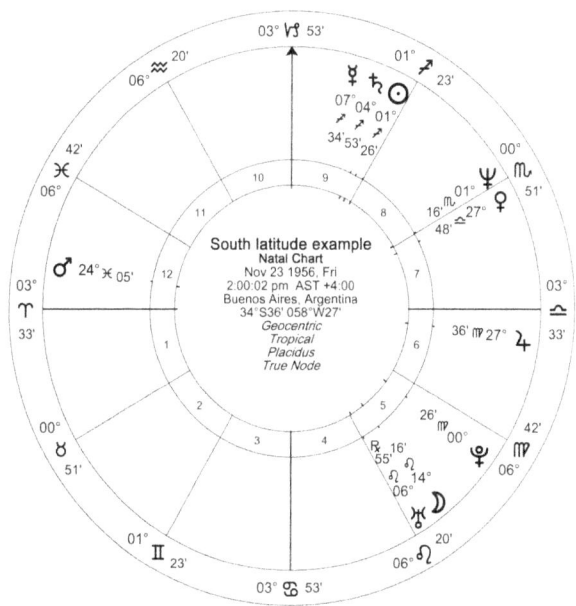

If the birthplace longitude is east of Greenwich, the GMT is calculated by adding the time correction for the meridian from Greenwich Mean Time.

EASTERN LONGITUDE BIRTH

The next calculation will be of a birth in Odessa, Ukraine, (formerly USSR), on February 14, 1960, at 6:00 AM EET, (Eastern European Time Zone was formerly Zone 1) at longitude 30°E 46 and latitude 46°N 30. Eastern European Time has a variance of two hours from Greenwich time. See Figure 18 for final chart.

Figure 18. Horoscope for eastern longitude example.

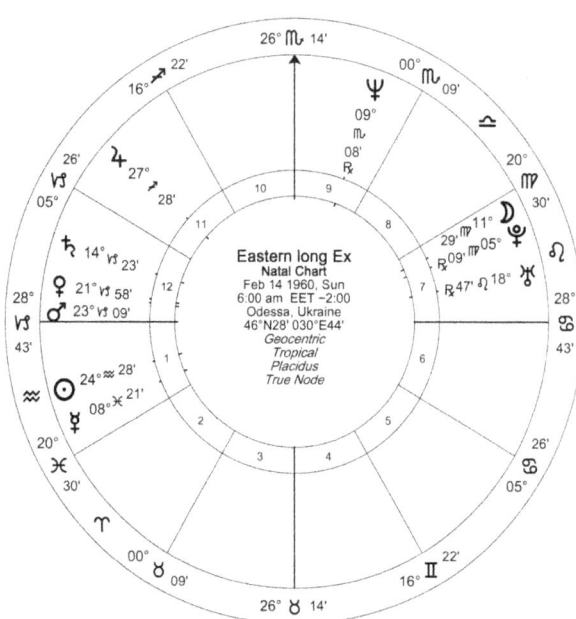

Other Factors in Creating the Horoscope

Birth Time:	6:00:00
Difference from Greenwich to EET:	−2:00:00
RESULT: Greenwich Mean Time:	4:00:00 GMT on Feb 14, 1960
Sidereal time for previous midnight:	9:32:07
Birth time interval from midnight:	+4:00:00
Correction for interval:	+ 00:39
RESULT: Greenwich Sidereal Time:	13:32:46
Longitude Correction (add for east):	+ 2:03:04
RESULT: Local Sidereal Time:	15:35:50 LST

SOUTHERN HEMISPHERE, EASTERN LONGITUDE BIRTH

To incorporate the information given about births in southern latitudes and births in eastern longitudes the next example will be a horoscope erected for a native born in Melbourne, Australia, on December 7, 1971, at 4:00 PM AEDT. The longitude of Melbourne is 144 E 58 with a latitude of 37 S 45. The time standard for that city is GST, or Guam Standard Time, which is the same as East Australia Standard Time. Melbourne was on Daylight or Summer Time during 1971:

Birth Time:	4:00:00 PM
Subtract one hour for daylight savings:	−1:00:00
Standard birth time:	3:00:00 PM
Add 12 hours for PM birth:	+12 hrs
	15:00:00
Time difference from Greenwich to GST:	−10 hrs

Greenwich Mean Time:	5:00:00 GMT
Sidereal time from previous midnight:	5:00:27
GMT birth time:	5:00:00
Correction for interval:	00:00:49
Add 12 hours for south latitude:	12:00:00
Greenwich Sidereal Time Raw Data:	22:00:76
Longitude correction (add for east:)	+9:39:52
Local Sidereal Time Raw Data:	31:39:128
Corrected:	31:41:08
More than one day, subtract 24 hours:	−24 hours
RESULT: Local Sidereal Time:	7:41:08

Figure 19. Horoscope for southern hemisphere, south latitude example.

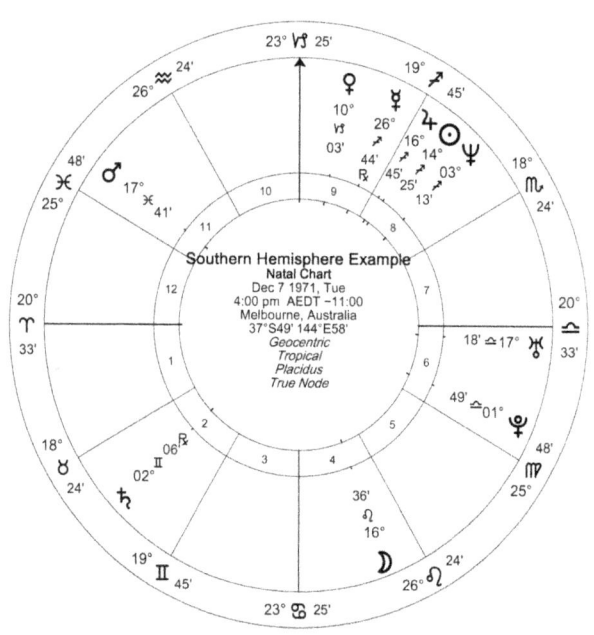

Other Factors in Creating the Horoscope

CALCULATION OF DECLINATION

At the beginning of the chapter we discussed declinations, and calculated the declination of the Sun for Female Child, from Chapter 5. Now it is time to practice the calculation of declinations further. Below is a declination table from an ephemeris, for November 1956, when our South Latitude example person from Buenos Aires was born.

Note that this table does not contain sidereal time or the nodes of the Moon, only declination positions.

Birth date:	November 23, 1956
Birth time:	2:00 PM AST
Birth location:	Buenos Aires, Argentina
Constant Multiplier:	.75

(Do you recall the procedure to calculate the constant multiplier?)

	☉	☾
Declination at midnight the day AFTER birth:	20°S 30'	10°N 33'
Declination at midnight the day OF birth:	20°S 18'	14°N 44'
Difference= 24 hour motion:	12'	–4° 11'
Multiply by constant:	x .75	x .75
RESULT:	09'	188
Add or Subtract from earlier date:	20°S 09'	188÷60=
		3.13
		.13x60=8
Subtract 3° 08' from Moon's position:		14°N 44'
Calculated Declination Interval:		– 3° 08'
RESULT:		11°N 36'

The Moon has more steps due to the number of degrees it covers in 24 hours. We had to SUBTRACT from the Moon's position because the Moon was moving toward the celestial equator, which is the same as moving southward. If you look further down the column of the Moon's declinations you will see that its declination becomes south on November 27. As mentioned earlier, with declinations it is common to have negative numbers, just be sure to indicate where subtraction is indicated.

	☿	♀
Declination at midnight the day AFTER birth:	22°S 53'	09°S 03'
Declination at midnight the day OF birth:	22°S 32'	08°S 37'
Difference= 24 hour motion:	21'	26'
Multiply by constant:	x .75	x .75
RESULT:	16'	20'
Add or Subtract from earlier date:	22°S 48	08°S 57'

You can see that the process is simple. We prepared the birth data to account for the time zone, calculated the GMT, and from that we calculated the constant multiplier used to determine the interval. That same interval is applied to planetary longitudes as well as declinations. For calculating the house cusps the constant is no longer based on planetary motion, but the location of the person for whom the chart is being created. We used the longitude and latitude to physically locate the native in order to place the planets within the house structure. This makes the house wheel with its cusps and planets a snapshot of the heavens at the native's location at the moment of birth.

Managing the calculations by keeping them in a tabular form as shown in these exercises will help to prevent errors. As you can clearly see, with all these numbers to manage, organization is critical, and also an easy habit to create with practice. As you practice these calculations you will readily see the benefit of careful notation and organization.

Work through the following calculations with what you've learned so far, and the finished charts will be at the end of the chapter. The outer planets may or may not need to be calculated due to their slow motion.

Birth date: June 21, 1976
Birth time: 5:12 PM EDT
Birth location: Pontiac, Michigan
Longitude & Latitude 83°W 17', 42°N 38'

Given birth time:	5:12 PM EDT
Subtract 1 hour for DST:	–1 hr
Local standard time:	4:12 PM
Add 12 hours for PM time:	+12 hrs
Local birth time:	16:12
Adjust for time zone (+west, –east):	+ 5 hrs
Greenwich birth time:	21:12

Calculate Constant: (12÷60=.20)   (21.2÷24=.88)

	☉	☾	☿	♀
6/22	0°♋42'	27°♈22'	8°♊57'	1°♋45'
6/21	29♊44'	15°♈34'	7°♊38'	0°♋31'
	58'	11° 48'	1° 19'	1° 14'
	x .88	11x60=660+48'	79'	74'
	51	708	x .88	x .88
	29♋44	x .88=	70'	65'
	+ 50'	623÷60=	7°♊38'	0°♋31'
	0°♋35'	10.38	+ 1° 10'	+ 1° 05
		(.38x60=23')	8°♊48'	1°♋36'
		15°♈ 34'		
		+ 10° 23'		
		25°♈57'		

Other Factors in Creating the Horoscope

A word of caution — Calculating planets and houses by hand versus using computer software to create a chart will often give numbers in the minutes and seconds columns that can be off by one minute, sometimes two, and the seconds by even more. Please do not worry about this – you are not doing the math incorrectly. Astrology software makes its calculations to more accurate degrees than what we are learning to do by hand. When the student is more advanced, there will be the opportunity to learn finer calculations than what we are initially learning here. When you check your work you will find that the created charts at the end of the chapter may have some minutes that are off by one or more.

If you are using astrology software, input this data into your own program and take note of any differences. Some astrology programs will show slightly different numbers in places. This is because calculations are made according to the software creator's preferences. More advanced work will often use decimals to the fifth place, where hand calculations will often round off to the second place. Practice using decimals to the fifth place and see how the results shift. As always, repetition helps to commit this process to memory, and you will become faster at calculating, and more accurate. Now onto declinations for the above chart:

	☉	☾	☿	♀
6/22	23°N26'	11°N43'	19°N16'	23°N50'
6/21	23°N26'	8°N13'	18°N54'	23°N48'
	0	3° 30'	22'	02'
		210' x .88=	22 x .88=	2 x .88=
		185'=3° 05'	19'	02'
		8°N13'	18°N54'	23°N48'
		+ 3° 05'	+ 19'	+ 02'
Final:	23°N26'	11°N 18'	19N13'	23°N02'

The Sun had no change in 24 hours, the Moon was typical in its movement, as was Mercury. With Venus the interval was such a low number that the constant barely registered any change. Venus' two minutes of movement multiplied by .88 gave a sum of 1.76, since .76 is more than three quarters of 100, we rounded the number up to two, which gave us the same number. This is not uncommon. Be sure, as always, to carefully note numbers that carry over to the next column, degrees that go over 30°, and hours that go beyond 24.

You will have birth time adjustments that carry over into the next day or the previous day, depending upon where in the world your calculations are for, and the time of day or night. This is important and must be noted carefully at the beginning of your calculations. One number off at the beginning will throw the whole endeavor off, and then time has been wasted. Double check the numbers, and *always use a calculator*.

One more example will be provided, but the calculations are up to the student. An ephemeris and declinations table for December 2000 are provided The final chart will be at the end of the chapter.

Birth date:	December 21, 2000
Birth time:	3:17 AM PST
Birth location:	Encinitas, CA
Long & Lat:	117°W 17', 33°N 02'

Given birth time:	3:17 AM PST
(No change for DST or PM time)	3:17 AM
Adjust for time zone (+west, −east)	+ 8 hrs
Greenwich birth time:	11:17 AM
Calculate constant:	.47

Interpolate the planets, then move onto calculation of the house cusp calculations with the following calculations:

Sidereal time at midnight birth date:	5:59:28
Greenwich birth time	11:17:00
Solar–Sidereal time correction:	00:01:51
Subtotal in raw data:	16:77:79
Longitude into time: (– west, + east)	–7:49:08
Total in raw data:	9:28:71
Final LST:	9:29:11
Greater listed sidereal time:	9h32m0s
Lesser listed sidereal time:	9h28m0s

By now you will have noticed that raw data is left in the columns until the calculations are finished. When the time correction is made for longitude there will be more addition or subtraction, and its easier, and less work make all adjustments with the final numbers. Now lets continue:

Subtract the lesser listed sidereal time from the LST:

LST:	9:29:11
Lesser listed sidereal time:	9:28:00
Sum:	00:01:11

$(11 \div 60 = .18)$ $\quad$ $(1.18 \div 4 = .30)$ Constant = .30

Finish calculating the houses for this birth data, then place the planets into their proper locations. Check your work against the charts at the end of the chapter. For any errors, go back over the math step by step and try to see where the numbers went off track. Work slowly and methodically, use good organization, and a calculator.

Places where errors are most likely to occur are in using mixed quantities, and keeping the columns straight. Each column is calculated separately. Also, birthdates that go into the following day can create confusion if the new date is not noted carefully. One of the most common errors is accidentally using the sidereal time for the Sun's position. Since sidereal time is listed to the left of the Sun column in the ephemeris, this happens all too often.

Important: when working with your planetary longitude numbers, you can check your progress easily by checking to see if the interval you have calculated matches the average motion of the planet in question. The numbers should make sense. If you are calculating the Moon and you get a daily motion that is less or more than average, your math is off. If your constant multiplier is not representative of the actual time period you need to calculate, check again, you have made an error. For example, if a person was born at 18:00 hours, (18:00 or 6 PM), and there are no minutes to decimalize, this gives a constant multiplier of .75, because this is literally 75% of a day. If this person was born at 6:00 AM, or 6:00 hours, the constant would be .25 because this is 25% of a day. As the student works with these numbers more and more, it will become second nature to recognize correct and incorrect calculations.

Review questions for Chapter 6:

1) What is declination?

2) Finish the chart for Encinitas, California and put all planets in proper houses, with Midheaven and Ascendant.

3) Calculate the declinations and note them for further study in the next chapter. Ephemeris and declinations tables for December 2000 are provided below.

DECEMBER 2000

☉ PARTIAL ECLIPSE, 04 ♑ 14, 25 DECEMBER, 17h 36m

LONGITUDE for 0h

Day Jour	S.T.	☉	☽	☿	♀	♂	♃	♄	⛢	♆	♇	☊ True
1 F	4 37 04	9♐ 08 50	4♒ 40 58	25♏ 37	21♐ 20	16♎ 27	6♉R 45	28♉R 34	17♒ 25	4♒ 23	12♑ 36	16♌ 57
2 Sa	4 40 44	10 09 50	16 27 50	27 08	22 31	17 04	05 37	28 29	17 27	4 24	12 38	15 56
3 Su	4 44 48	11 10 32	28 18 47	28 41	23♐ 42	17 17	05 29	28 25	17 31	4 24	12 40	15 00
4 M	4 48 52	12 11 27	10♓ 10 55	0♐ 14	24 53	17 18	05 21	28 20	17 33	4 24	12 43	15R 01
5 T	4 52 56	13 12 17	22 06 48	1 48	26 03	18 11	05 15	28 15	17 35	4 24	12 45	14 59
6 W	4 56 00	14 13 10	4♈ 08 39	3 19	27 14	18 46	05 09	28 11	17 37	4 24	12 47	14 55
7 Th	5 00 04	15 14 08	16 18 05	4 48	28 24	19 21	05 04	28 06	17 39	4 24	12 50	14 51
8 F	5 04 08	16 15 07	28 36 28	6 19	29 34	19 57	04 59	28 02	17 41	4 24	12 52	14 48
9 Sa	5 08 12	17 16 07	11♉ 05 56	7 58	0♑ 44	20 41	04 55	27 58	17 43	4 24	12 54	14 48
10 Su	5 12 16	18 17 08	23 53 28	9 11	01 54	21 17	04 53	25 53	17 45	4 25	12 57	14D 42
11 M	5 16 20	19 18 09	6♊ 52 34	10 49	03 04	22 06	04 51	25 49	17 45	4 24	13 13	14 38
12 T	5 20 23	20 19 10	20 14 52	12 22	04 14	22 41	04 49	25 41	17 47	4 24	13 16	14 38
13 W	5 24 27	21 20 11	3♋ 52 39	13 54	05 24	23 17	04 48	25 32	17 49	4 24	13 20	14 38
14 Th	5 28 31	22 21 13	17 46 08	15 45	06 33	23 53	04 48	25 26	17 52	4 24	13 24	14 37
15 F	5 32 35	23 22 15	1♌ 53 18	17 18	07 43	24 29	04D 48	25 25	17 54	4 24	13 26	14 36
16 Sa	5 36 39	24 23 17	16 12 04	18 52	08 52	25 05	04 48	25 21	17 57	4 24	13 28	14 32
17 Su	5 40 43	25 24 20	0♍ 42 12	20 25	10 01	25 41	04 49	25 15	17 58	4 24	13 30	14 30
18 M	5 44 47	26 25 23	15 25 03	21 58	11 10	26 18	04 51	25 15	18 01	4 25	13 34	14 28
19 T	5 48 51	27 26 27	0♎ 09 52	23 32	12 19	26 54	04 53	25 10	18 02	4 25	13 37	14 38
20 W	5 52 55	28 27 30	14 22 53	25 06	13 28	27 30	04 55	25 06	18 04	4 25	13 41	14 38
21 Th	5 55 59	29 28 34	29 10 53	25 41	14 37	28 03	04 57	25 02	18 06	4 25	14 00	14 37
22 F	6 00 01	0♑ 29 38	13♏ 14 11	28 16	15 45	28 43	05 00	24 55	18 08	4 25	14 12	14 34
23 Sa	6 04 00	1 30 42	27 37 04	29 52	16 54	29 19	05 04	24 57	18 11	4 25	14 15	14 32
24 Su	6 08 11	2 31 47	13♐ 17 28	1 29	18 02	29 55	05 07	24 47	18 17	4 25	14 18	14 30
25 M	6 12 15	3 32 52	25 26 12	3 07	19 10	0♏ 31	05 11	24 43	18 22	4 25	14 31	14 28
26 T	6 16 18	4 33 57	7♑ 29 10	4 46	20 18	01 08	05 15	24 38	18 26	4 25	14 37	14 28
27 W	6 20 22	5 35 03	19 19 10	6 27	21 25	01 45	05 19	24 47	18 30	4 25	14 35	14 28
28 Th	6 24 26	6 36 08	1♒ 13 10	8 10	22 32	02 21	05 24	24 41	18 30	4 25	14 40	14 28
29 F	6 28 31	7 37 14	13 24 19	9 55	23 38	02 57	05 30	24 38	18 33	4 25	14 40	14 34
30 Sa	6 32 34	8 38 21	25 02 48	11 40	24 45	03 34	05 35	24 41	18 36	4 25	14 42	14 32
31 Su	6 36 38	9♑ 39 28	6♓ 42 32	12♑ 39	25♑ 52	04♏ 21	5♉ 56	24♉R 38	18♒ 38	4♒ 26	13♑ 44	14♌ 31

Grant Textbook Series, Vol. III 111

Above: Declination table for December 2000

Previous page: Ephemeris table for December, 2000.

Other Factors in Creating the Horoscope

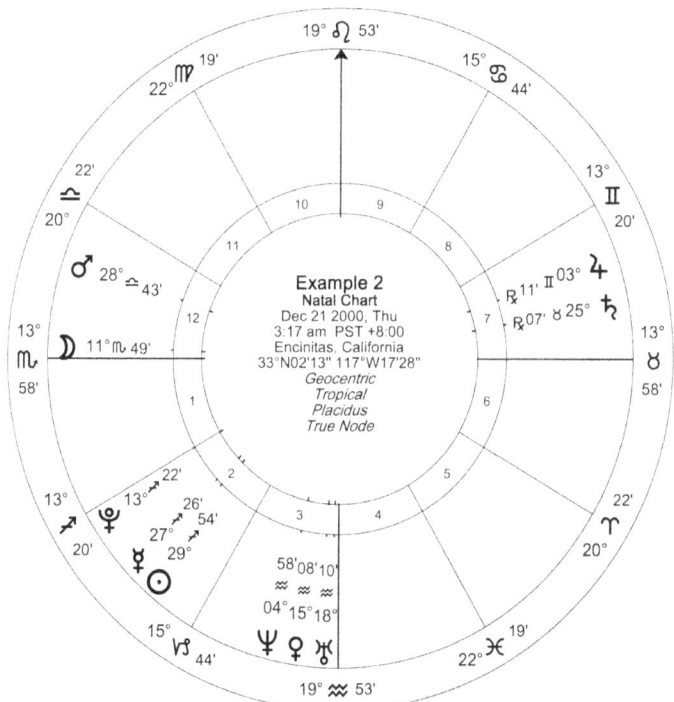

Completed natal chart, or horoscope for a birth in Encinitas, California, December 21, 2000.
You may have slight differences in the minutes columns, as all charts in this volume were made with computer software, which calculates much more precisely.

| Chapter 7 |

Alternative Method Of Chart Calculation

There are various methods of calculating the horoscope, and in this chapter we will explore another procedure. This method uses Diurnal Proportional Logarithms. It was the preferred method of calculation for many years, and is still in use by many. This example uses a noon ephemeris. In the following example the birth was on November 7, 1930 at 11:00 AM EST in New York City.

Birth Time:	11 :00:00 AM
Time Zone Differential:	+ 5:00:00
RESULT: Greenwich mean time of birth:	16:00:00 GMT
Correction for noon ephemeris:	+12:00:00
Raw data	28:00:00
Subtract 24 hours – more than one day	–24:00:00

RESULT: GMT with noon ephemeris 4:00:00 on November 7, 1930 –the birth occurred 4 hours **after** the noon ephemeris time.

TABLE OF PROPORTION LOGARITHMS
Hours or Degrees

Min.	0	1	2	3	4	5	6	7	8	9	10	11
0	3.1584	1.3802	1.0792	9031	7781	6812	6021	5351	4771	4260	3802	3388
1	3.1584	3730	0756	07	63	6798	09	41	62	52	3795	82
2	2.8573	3660	0720	8983	45	84	5997	30	53	44	88	75
3	.6812	3590	0685	59	28	69	85	20	44	36	80	68
4	.5563	3522	0649	8935	10	55	73	10	35	28	73	62
5	2.4594	1.3454	1.0614	8912	7692	6741	5961	5300	4726	4220	3766	3355
6	.3802	3388	0580	8888	74	26	49	5269	17	12	59	49
7	.3133	3323	0546	65	57	12	37	79	08	04	52	42
8	.2553	3258	0511	42	39	6698	25	69	4699	4196	45	36
9	.2041	3195	0478	19	22	84	13	59	90	88	38	29
10	2.1584	1.3133	1.0444	8796	7604	6670	5902	5249	4682	4180	3730	3323
11	.1170	3071	0411	73	7587	56	5890	39	73	72	23	16
12	.0792	.3010	.0378	51	70	42	78	29	64	64	16	10
13	.0444	.2950	.0345	28	52	28	66	19	55	56	09	03
14	.0122	.2891	.0313	06	35	14	55	09	46	49	02	3297
15	1.9823	1.2833	1.0280	8683	7518	6600	5843	5199	4638	4141	3695	3291
16	.9542	.2775	.0248	61	01	6587	32	89	29	33	88	84
17	.9279	.2719	.0216	39	7484	73	20	79	20	25	81	78
18	.9031	.2663	.0185	17	67	59	09	69	11	17	74	71
19	.8796	.2607	.0153	8595	51	46	5797	59	03	09	67	65
20	1.8573	1.2553	1.0122	8573	7434	6532	5786	5149	4594	4102	3660	3258
21	.8361	.2499	.0091	52	17	19	74	39	85	4094	53	52
22	.8159	.2445	.0061	30	01	05	63	29	77	86	46	46
23	.7966	.2393	.0030	09	7384	6492	52	20	68	79	39	39
24	.7781	.2341	1.0000	8487	68	78	40	10	59	71	32	33
25	1.7604	1.2289	0.9970	8466	7351	6465	5729	5100	4551	4063	3625	3227
26	.7434	.2239	.9940	45	35	51	18	5090	42	55	18	20
27	.7270	.2188	.9910	24	18	38	06	81	34	48	11	14
28	.7112	.2139	.9881	03	02	25	5695	71	25	40	04	08
29	.6960	.2090	.9852	8382	7286	12	84	61	16	32	3597	01
30	1.6812	1.2041	0.9823	8361	7270	6398	5673	5051	4508	4025	3590	3195
31	.6670	.1993	.9794	41	54	85	62	42	4499	17	83	89
32	.6532	.1946	.9765	21	38	72	51	32	91	10	77	83
33	.6398	.1899	.9737	00	22	59	40	23	82	02	70	76
34	.6269	.1852	.9708	8279	06	46	29	13	74	3995	63	70
35	1.6143	1.1806	0.9680	8259	7190	6333	5618	5003	4466	3987	3555	3164
36	.6021	.1761	.9652	39	74	20	07	4994	57	79	49	57
37	.5902	.1716	.9625	19	59	07	5596	84	49	72	42	51
38	.5786	.1671	.9597	8199	43	6294	85	75	40	64	35	45
39	.5673	.1627	.9570	79	28	82	74	65	32	57	29	39
40	1.5563	1.1584	0.9542	8159	7112	6269	5563	4956	4424	3949	3522	3133
41	.5456	.1540	.9515	40	7097	56	52	47	15	42	15	26
42	.5351	.1498	.9488	20	81	43	41	37	07	34	08	20
43	.5249	.1455	.9462	01	66	31	31	28	4399	27	01	14
44	.5149	.1413	.9435	8081	50	18	20	18	90	19	3495	08
45	1.5051	1.1372	0.9409	8062	7035	6205	5509	4909	4382	3912	3488	3102
46	.4956	.1331	.9383	43	20	6193	5498	00	74	05	81	3096
47	.4863	.1290	.9356	23	05	80	88	4890	65	3897	75	89
48	.4771	.1249	.9330	04	6990	68	77	81	57	90	68	83
49	.4682	.1209	.9305	7985	75	55	66	72	49	82	61	77
50	1.4594	1.1170	0.9279	7966	6960	6143	5456	4863	4341	3875	3455	3071
51	.4508	.1130	.9254	47	45	31	45	53	33	68	48	65
52	.4424	.1091	.9228	29	30	18	35	44	24	60	41	59
53	.4341	.1053	.9203	10	15	06	24	35	16	53	35	53
54	.4260	.1015	.9178	7891	00	6094	14	26	08	46	28	47
55	1.4180	1.0977	0.9153	7873	6885	6081	5403	4817	4300	3838	3421	3041
56	.4102	.0939	.9128	54	71	69	5393	08	4292	31	15	35
57	.4025	.0902	.9104	36	56	57	82	4799	84	24	08	28
58	.3949	.0865	.9079	18	41	45	72	89	76	17	01	22
59	.3875	.0828	.9055	00	27	33	61	80	68	09	3395	16

The table of Diurnal Proportional Logarithms is carried to the fourth decimal place. These logarithm tables are calculated on a 24 hour basis. If desired, the top horizontal line can be considered minutes and the left-hand column as seconds, since they are both derived from divisions of 60. (See Table 8.)

Find the logarithm for four hours in the column headed

TABLE OF PROPORTION LOGARITHMS
Hours or Degrees

Min.	12	13	14	15	16	17	18	19	20	21	22	23
0	3010	2663	2341	2041	1761	1498	1249	1015	0792	0580	0378	0185
1	04	57	36	36	56	93	45	11	88	77	75	82
2	2998	52	30	32	52	89	41	07	85	73	71	79
3	92	46	25	27	47	85	37	03	81	70	68	75
4	86	41	20	22	43	81	34	0999	77	66	64	72
5	2980	2635	2315	2017	1738	1476	1229	0996	0774	0563	0361	0169
6	74	29	10	12	34	72	25	92	70	59	58	66
7	68	24	05	08	29	68	21	88	66	56	55	63
8	62	18	00	03	25	64	17	84	63	52	52	60
9	56	13	2295	1998	20	60	13	80	59	49	48	57
10	2950	2607	89	1993	1716	1455	1209	0977	0756	0546	0345	0153
11	45	02	84	89	11	51	05	73	52	42	42	50
12	38	2596	79	84	07	47	01	69	49	39	39	47
13	33	91	74	79	02	43	1197	65	45	35	35	44
14	27	85	69	74	1698	38	93	62	42	32	32	41
15	2921	2580	2264	1969	1694	1434	1189	0958	0738	0529	0329	0138
16	15	75	59	65	89	30	85	54	34	25	26	35
17	09	69	54	60	85	26	82	50	31	22	22	32
18	03	64	49	55	80	22	78	47	27	18	19	29
19	2897	58	44	50	76	17	74	43	24	15	16	25
20	2891	2553	2239	1946	1671	1413	1170	0939	0720	0511	0313	0122
21	85	47	34	41	67	09	66	35	17	08	09	19
22	80	42	29	36	63	05	62	32	13	05	06	16
23	74	36	23	32	58	01	58	28	09	01	03	13
24	68	31	18	27	54	1397	54	24	06	0498	00	10
25	2862	2526	2213	1922	1649	1393	1150	0920	0702	0495	0296	0107
26	56	20	08	17	45	88	46	17	0699	91	92	04
27	50	15	03	13	40	84	42	13	95	88	90	01
28	45	09	2198	08	36	80	38	09	92	85	87	0098
29	39	04	93	03	32	76	34	05	88	81	83	94
30	2833	2499	2188	1899	1627	1372	1130	0902	0685	0478	0280	0091
31	27	93	83	94	23	68	26	0898	81	74	77	88
32	21	88	78	90	19	63	23	94	78	71	74	85
33	16	83	73	85	14	59	19	91	74	68	71	82
34	10	77	68	80	10	55	15	87	70	64	67	79
35	2804	2472	2164	1875	1605	1351	1111	0883	0667	0461	0264	0076
36	2798	67	59	71	01	47	07	80	64	58	61	73
37	93	61	54	66	1597	43	03	76	60	54	58	70
38	87	56	49	62	92	39	1099	72	56	51	55	67
39	81	51	44	57	88	35	95	68	53	48	51	64
40	2775	2445	2139	1852	1584	1331	1092	0865	0649	0444	0248	0061
41	70	40	34	48	79	27	88	61	46	41	45	58
42	64	35	29	43	75	22	84	57	42	37	42	55
43	58	30	24	38	71	18	80	54	39	34	39	52
44	53	24	19	34	66	14	76	50	35	31	35	48
45	2747	2419	2114	1829	1562	1310	1072	0846	0632	0428	0232	0045
46	41	14	09	25	58	06	68	43	29	24	29	42
47	36	09	04	20	53	02	64	39	25	21	26	39
48	30	03	2099	16	49	1298	61	35	21	18	23	36
49	24	2398	2095	11	45	94	57	32	18	14	20	33
50	2719	2393	2090	1806	1540	1290	1053	0828	0614	0411	0216	0030
51	13	88	85	02	36	86	49	24	11	08	13	27
52	07	82	80	1797	32	82	45	21	08	04	10	24
53	02	77	75	93	28	78	41	17	04	01	07	21
54	2696	72	70	88	23	74	37	14	01	0398	04	18
55	2691	2367	2065	1784	1519	1270	1034	0810	0597	0394	0201	0015
56	85	62	61	79	15	66	30	06	94	91	97	12
57	79	56	56	74	10	61	26	03	90	88	94	09
58	74	51	51	70	06	57	22	0799	87	84	91	06
59	68	46	46	65	02	53	18	95	83	81	88	03

"4", on the top line marked "0" = 0.7781. This is called the Constant Logarithm or the Logarithm of Interval and is used to calculate each planet's position.

The birth occurred before noon, at Greenwich it occurred between noon of November 7 and noon of November 8. This

Alternative Methods of Chart Calculation

is repeated for the sake of emphasis: the time of birth must be calculated for Greenwich since that is the place for which the ephemeris gives the positions of the planets.

Hence the Sun, the Moon, and each planet will be at some point between the positions given in the ephemeris for noon of November 7 and noon November 8. Reference to a 1930 ephemeris will show that the Sun was at 14 ♏ 22 at noon on November 7 and at 15 ♏ 22 at noon on November 8, GMT. The Sun, therefore, appeared to move 1 degree in 24 hours.

If a midnight ephemeris had been used, the Sun's motion would have been given for midnight to midnight, and the calculation would have been made, not for four hours, but for the 16 hours between midnight of November 7, GMT, and the time of birth.

Reminder: it is usually possible to level off the Sun's motion to minutes; if less than 30 seconds drop, but if more than 30 seconds count to the next full minute. However, this should not be done in very precise work, as the calculation of a solar return horoscope would be made erroneous by this rounding off.

Reference to table 8 will show that the logarithm of 1 degree 00 minutes is 1.3802. Add this number to the logarithm of interval, or the constant logarithm, 0.7781, to get the sum of 2.1583. The logarithm in the table which is nearest this number will be the logarithm of the Sun's motion in four hours on that day. In the column headed "0", scroll down the column and find 10 minutes; this logarithm is found to be 2.1584; so, in this case the calculated logarithm and the logarithm nearest to it are almost exactly the same number.

Therefore, since the Sun moved 10 minutes during the four hours from noon, GMT, before birth occurred, this motion is added to the Sun's position at noon, GMT, before birth, i.e., 14♏21'30". The position thus found being 14♏31'30" or 14♏32. This is the Sun's position at the moment of birth, and it is entered in its proper place on the chart. It will benefit you a great deal to organize your data into tabular form for accuracy in calculations. Double check all mathematical steps for errors. In this horoscope the Sun at 14°♏32' will be found in house X, (10) approaching the Midheaven, (MC).

Lets do the Moon's calculations next. Note: Gemini is the third sign and Taurus is the second. Since there are 30 degrees in each sign, the Moon has moved through the remaining degrees of Taurus into Gemini. To subtract, borrow a full sign of 30 degrees and add to it the 10 degrees and 38 minutes into Gemini, as follows:

10♊37 = 40♊38
27♉15 = 27♉15
                13° 23' = 24 hour motion

MOON Calculations		Logarithm
Longitude AFTER birth, Nov 8	10♊37	
Longitude BEFORE birth, Nov 7	24♉15	
RESULT: 24–hour motion	13° 23'	= .2536
Constant log for 4 hour interval		= .7781
RESULT: Moon's motion in 4 hours in logarithm		1.0317
Log reduced to degrees (increment of correction)		2° 14'
Add to Moon position on November 7		27♉15'
RESULT: Moon's position at birth		29°♉29'

MERCURY Calculations		Logarithm
Longitude AFTER birth, Nov 8	16♏12	
Longitude BEFORE birth, Nov 7	14♏36	
RESULT: 24–hour motion	1° 36'	= 1.1761
Constant log for 4 hour interval		.7781

RESULT: Mercury's motion in 4 hours in logarithm 1.9542

Log reduced to degrees (increment of correction)   16'

Add to Mercury position on Nov 7   14♏36

RESULT: Mercury's position at birth   14°♏52'

VENUS Calculations	Logarithm

Longitude AFTER birth, Nov 8   6♐34 Rx

Longitude BEFORE birth, Nov 7   6♐49 Rx

RESULT: 24–hour motion   – 15' = 1.9823

Constant log for 4 hour interval   = 0.7781

RESULT: Venus' motion in 4 hours in logarithm   2.7604

Log reduced to degrees (increment of correction) –03'

Subtract from Venus' position on Nov. 7   6♐48 Rx

                                                – 03'

RESULT: Venus's position at birth   6♐45 Rx

The birth position of Mars, found in the same manner is 7°♌52. The remaining planets – Jupiter, Saturn, Uranus, Neptune, and Pluto – move so slowly that their positions need not be calculated logarithmically. They can be calculated to the nearest minute of longitude by approximating the time interval between noon and the GMT of birth and taking that fraction of the 24 hour motion. The positions of these major exterior planets are given for noon, November 7, 4:00 PM is four hours after noon, or one-sixth of the 24 hour interval. Thus, one–sixth of the 24 hour motion in minutes is added to each planet (or subtracted if the planet is retrograde) as follows:

Jupiter: 20♎31 and moves no distance in 24 hours – at birth 20♎31.

Saturn: 7°♑51 and moves 5 minutes in 24 hours – at birth 7°♑56.

Uranus: 12°♈14 Rx and moves 2 minutes in 24 hours – at birth 12♈12 Rx.

Neptune: 5♍30 and moves 1 minute in 24 hours – at birth 5♍31.

Pluto: 20♎50 Rx and moves 0 minutes in 24 hours – at birth 20♎50 Rx.

For further experience create the following chart and check the results against the charts given at the end of this chapter.

EXAMPLE CHART CALCULATIONS
Midnight Ephemeris
July 4, 1976

Washington D.C. 77° W 02', 38° N 54'

8:07 AM EDT

We will begin with the steps from the first method of calculation presented in Chapter 5. (The student can use either method presented, and check against the charts at the end of the chapter.)

Birth Time	8:07:00 AM EDT
Adjust to standard time	– 1 hr
	7:07 AM
Adjust for Time Zone	+ 5 hrs
Birth at Greenwich Mean Time	12:07 PM

Remember – do NOT add 12 hours for PM time in this case. This rule does not come into effect until the time hits 1:00 PM. The above time is written as 12 hours and 7 minutes after midnight, or an interval of 12 hours and 7 minutes.

Decimalize time and obtain constant multiplier

$\quad$ 7 ÷ 60 = .12 $\qquad$ 12.12 ÷ 24 = .51 Constant

We will calculate the Sun's position and declination, and you can practice with the rest of the planets:

Sun Longitude:

Sun July 5 midnight:	13°♋06
Sun July 4 midnight	–12°♋09 Logarithm: 0.2956
24 Hour Motion	57' Logarithm: 1.4025
Add to July 4 longitude:	1.6981
Interval in 12h 07m	logarithm = 29'
Add to Sun's position on July 4	12°♋09
	+ 29'=
Sun's final position	12°♋38'

Sun Declination:

Sun July 5	22 N 48
Sun July 4	22 N 53
Alert! Negative number!	–05
Multiply by constant	x .51
Interval of declination	–03
Subtract interval from Sun's position on July 4	22° N 53
	– 03
Sun's declination on July 4	22° N 50

HOUSE CUSP CALCULATION EXAMPLE

Previously, we adjusted the Example birth time to 12:07 PM

Greenwich Mean Time, or GMT. If you recall, we need to work with this time some more in order to calculate the house cusps. The next step is obtaining sidereal time at midnight day of birth, and the local sidereal time for the native. *Remember – we never round up or down with sidereal time.*

Sidereal time at midnight July 4	18:48:31
GMT birth time	12:07:00
Solar–Sidereal time correction	+00:01:59
Subtotal	30:56:90
Longitude into time (–W, + E)	– 5:08:08
Local Sidereal Time	25:49:22
More than one day, subtract 24 hours	–24 hrs
Local Sidereal Time	1:49:22

In the Table of Houses you should find the above LST in between the time blocks of 1h 48m 0s and 1h 52m 0s. Note also that the MC for these times has a range from 29°♈02'47"and 0°♉05'39". You will have to add 30°to the sign of Taurus in order to calculate the MC. The rest of the calculation should fall into line normally.

While we're on the subject of the MC, this is a great place for a spot check on how we have done with our time calculations so far. When the student gets to the point of determining the Local Sidereal Time, which we have just finished, get out the Table of Houses and go to the page or pages with your greater and lesser listed sidereal times to see where the MC falls. In the example charts at the end of the chapter you will be able to see quickly if the MC for your LST falls within the range of the greater and lesser listed sidereal times. If not, go back and check your work. Don't get discouraged if you make mistakes! Errors are frustrating, but you can always learn something from them, and with practice you will get better and better!

Next, we must find the constant multiplier. Do you recall that procedure? The student can find this one, finish the calculations and check the work against the example chart at the end of the chapter.

Good luck with your calculations!

Review questions for Chapter 7:

1. What is a diurnal logarithm table?

2. Create a natal chart for a person born December 11, 2000, in Encinitas, CA, at 9:02 AM, PST using the ephemeris and declination tables provided in the previous chapter. This is a midnight ephemeris. Try your calculations with either or both methods of calculation. The finished chart is at the end of the chapter to check your work. No peeking!

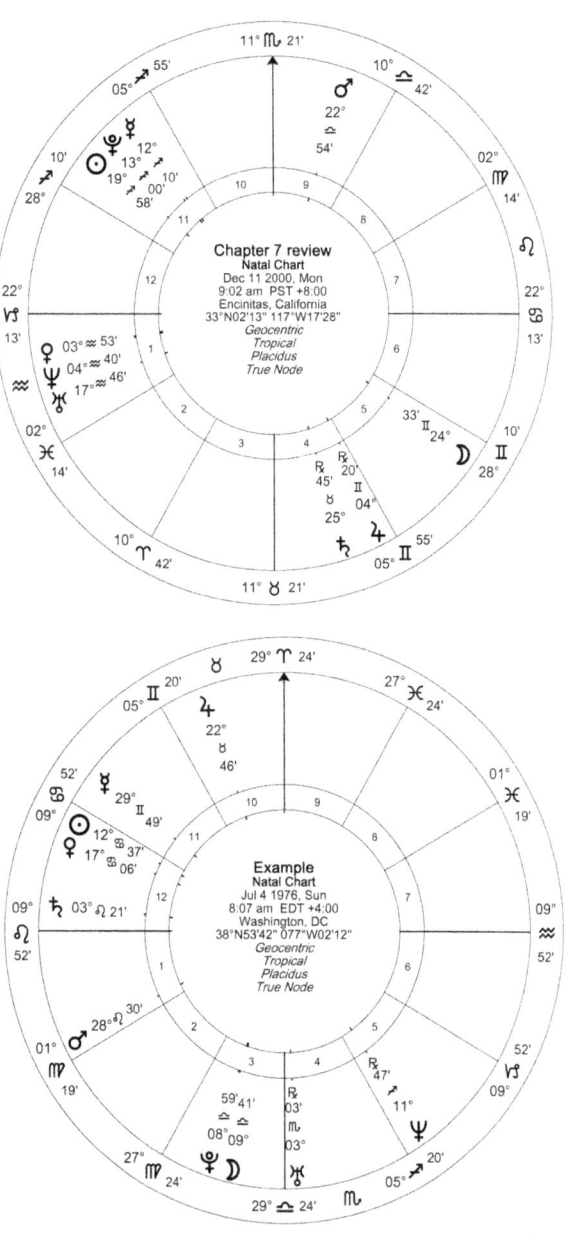

Alternative Methods of Chart Calculation

Chapter 8

Aspects

OF GREAT IMPORTANCE IN THE INTERPRETATION of horoscopes are the relative positions of the celestial bodies with respect to one another, and to certain sensitive points in the horoscope. In a natal chart these relative positions are called Aspects, and in a progressed chart Progressions or Direction. They are nothing more than the planets' distances from one another measured in longitude along the zodiac and are usually expressed in degrees.

Aspect	Distance in Zodiac	Symbol	Nature	Keyword	Orb
Conjunction	0°	☌	Variable	Preeminence	8°-10°
Semi–sextile	30°	⚹	Favorable	Growth	1° 2°
Semi-square	45°	∠	Unfavorable	Friction	2° 3°
Sextile	60°	✶	Favorable	Opportunity	5° 6°
Square	90°	□	Unfavorable	Obstacle	6° 8°
Trine	120°	△	Favorable	Ease	6° 8°
Sesquiquadrate	135°	⚼	Unfavorable	Agitation	2° 3°
Quincunx	150°	⚻	Difficult	Adjustment	1° 2°

(Quincunx is also known as Inconjunct.)

| Opposition | 180° | ☍ | Conflict | Separation | 8° 10° |
| Parallel | | ∥ | Variable | Intensity | 1° 2° |

As there is always research and discovery in the field of astrology, and over time other aspects have been discovered to have an influence. Much has been revealed and written about these aspects, and for the most part they are considered to be minor, and range from somewhat specialized, to highly specialized degrees. These aspects are the biquintile 144°, tredecile 108°, quintile 72°, and decile 36°, are used by many, but not all astrologers. Aspects like the decile, tredecile and quindecile are less common in use, and point to more specialized traits. Astrologer George J. McCormack has called attention to the divisions of 15 degrees, (15°, 75°, and 165°), in his limited research.

Selection of the above aspects was not an arbitrary matter: they are based upon certain very definite esoteric principles, and their value has been proven empirically through many centuries of use. The major aspects given by Ptolemy are: conjunction, sextile, trine, square, opposition, and parallel. Our knowledge of the minor aspects (the remaining ones in the above table) is from Kepler and the other great medieval astrologers.

It would take too long to explain the esoteric principles upon which these aspects are based, but these are discussed in the author's work on esoteric astrology as well as in any good textbook on the subject.

The student should be cautioned at the outset to avoid falling into the unhappy position of many other astrologers who attempt to fit all interpretation into the aspects indicated in the chart. While most people with very few aspects in their natal charts do not lead very eventful lives, others are able to overcome the inharmonious aspects given in their charts and show much development. In the same way, charts with a majority of favorable aspects may work out inharmoniously because of either house or sign position or because of lack of balance in the chart, while those with a majority of unfavorable aspects may often work out harmoniously. The following are the major steps to be followed in judging a horoscope:

First: group the zodiacal significations, such as quadruplicities, triplicities, quadrants, trinities, etc.

Second: find the house significations as indicated by the house placement of the zodiacal signs.

Third: determine the distribution of the planets themselves by signs and houses.

Fourth: ascertain the aspects between the celestial bodies and the sensitive points of the horoscope.

Fifth: determine the significations of the houses of the horoscope, as through them the aspects are expressed. In other words, they are the avenues in experience through which the other four categories operate.

It is seen from the above that the aspects are not, as so often indicated, of the first order of importance in interpreting the horoscope, but only fourth.

The conjunction and parallel of declination are not really aspects at all. The conjunction occurs when two planets occupy the same longitude degree of the zodiac (Figures 20 and 21), and the parallel of declination is formed when two or more planets are equidistant from the celestial equator or in the same declination, either north or south, when one planet is north and the other south. The declination of each planet is given in the

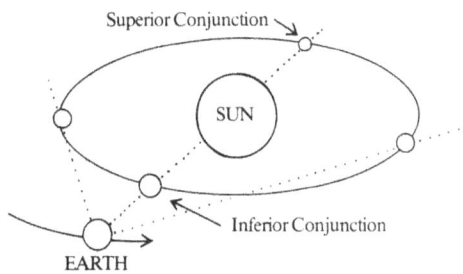

Figure 20. Formation of a conjunction by a planet within the orbit of Earth.

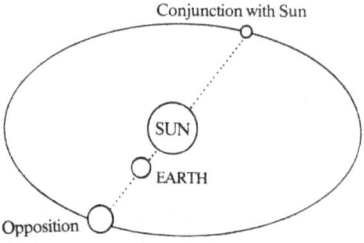

Figure 21. Formation of a conjunction by a planet outside the orbit of Earth.

ephemeris and may be calculated in the same manner as longitudinal position, using the same constant logarithm.

As already indicated, the major aspects are conjunction, sextile, square, trine, and opposition, and each of these must always be considered very carefully, It is also good to consider the parallel of declination a major factor, since it proves to be a strong influence in many horoscopes, In advanced interpretation all aspects vary in different charts to such a degree as to make their consideration confusing for the beginner.

The aspects which are at right angles to one another (as with the lines connecting 45°, 90°, 135°, 180°, 270°, and 360° of a circle on Figure 22) are unfavorable, in harmonious, or difficult. These are: square, opposition, and semi-square. On the other hand, those aspects which form a triangle (as with the lines connecting 30°, 60°, 120°, 240°, and 360° of a circle on Figure 23) are favorable, harmonious, or benefic. These are trine, sextile, and semi-sextile.

The determination of aspects is relatively simple, as they are only the number of longitudinal degrees of zodiac between two or more bodies, measured either forward or backward. When two planets are aspecting, the (lesser) faster moving planet is said to be **Applying** to the (greater) slower moving planet when the

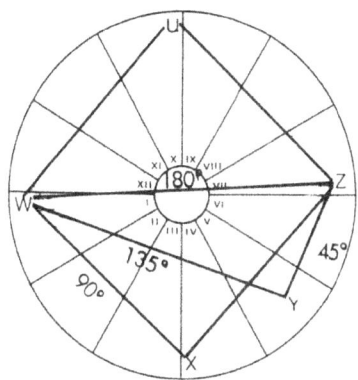

*Figure 22. Aspects at right angles to each other:
W to X is Square; W to Z is Opposition; W to Y is sesquiquadrate;
Y to Z is Semi-square; W, X, Z and U form a Grand Square.*

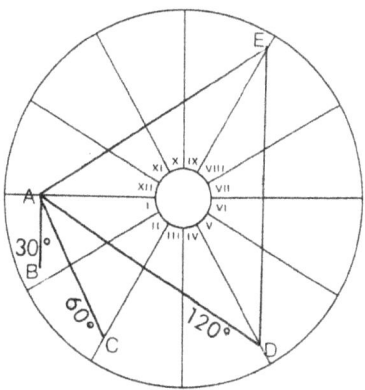

*Figure 23. Aspects which form a triangle together. A to B is
semi-sextile; A to C is sextile; A to D and E are trines; A, D and E
form a complete triangle, or Grand Trine.*

aspect is approaching, but not yet exact. The aspect will become exact at a later date due to the faster motion of the lesser planet. The lesser planet is always the one closer to the Sun and thus moving more rapidly; since the Moon is the fastest moving celestial body, it is the least. When the exact degree of the aspect has been passed, the lesser, or faster planet is said to be **Separating** from the greater, or slower moving planet.

For example, if the position of Mercury is 10♑ and that of Uranus is 15♉, these planets are 115 degrees of longitude apart. Because of Mercury's swifter motion, at some future time they will be exactly 120 degrees apart, and Mercury is therefore said to be applying to a trine of Uranus. If, however, Mercury were in 20♑ and Uranus in 15♉, they would be 125 degrees apart; the exact trine of 120 degrees would have been passed, and Mercury would be said to be separating from the trine aspect. An aspect applying to its exactness is always stronger than one separating from this position.

As already stated, aspects are either calculated forward in the zodiac, as from Aries to Gemini, or backward, as from Gemini to Aries. When calculated forward they are known as **Dexter aspects** and when calculated backward, **Sinister aspects**. Sinister aspects are slightly stronger for good or evil than dexter aspects.

In the example given, Mercury at 10♑ is the lesser or faster planet forming an aspect to Uranus at 15♉. Since the planet making application, Mercury, is ahead of the other planet this aspect must be calculated backward in the zodiac and is, therefore, an applying sinister trine aspect. An example of an applying dexter square aspect would be the Moon at 15♓ to Venus at 18♊. Two separating dexter aspects are Sun at 20♉ to Mars at 15♈, and Jupiter at 5♏ to Saturn at 2♎ (see Figures 24 and 25).

Mutual application of two celestial bodies occurs when the planet applied to is in retrograde motion. In such a case they are apparently traveling toward one another from opposite directions. For example, assume that the Moon is at 5♎ and Saturn at 10♒, retrograde. They are said to be in mutual trine to one another. Similarly, planets are in **Mutual Reception** when each is in the sign ruled by the other, as for example: Mars in Cancer

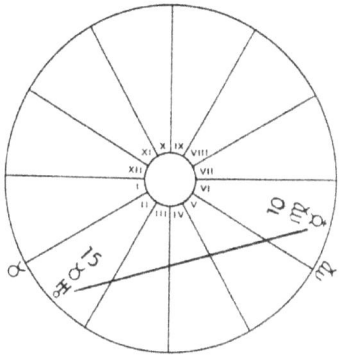

Figure 24. Mercury and Uranus forming an applying sinister trine aspect.

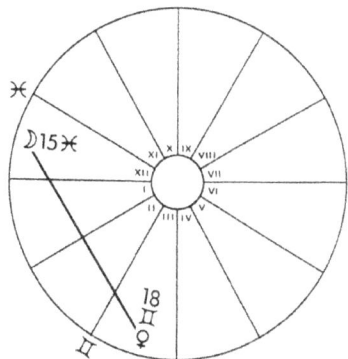

Figure 25. The Moon and Venus forming a dexter square aspect.

trine to the Moon in Scorpio or, more precisely, the Moon in Scorpio trine to Mars in Cancer (since the Moon moves faster). If the Moon were in Libra square to Mars in Cancer, we would say that the Moon **Disposes** of Mars.

If the planets in aspects were exactly the requisite number

of degrees apart, the whole matter would be greatly simplified. But this is not the case, since each planet has a **Body of Orb**. In the case of major aspects limit the allowance for orbs to no more than that given in the table, although narrower orbs are wiser. It is suggested that for major aspects an 8 degree orb for the planets, Sun and Moon be used, in other words, allow 82 to 98 degrees for the square, 112 to 128 degrees for the trine, etc. The closer the aspect is to exact, the stronger its influence will be. As you continue to learn, you will no doubt observe that some astrologers use a wider orb, 10° being fairly common. However, tighter orbs are wiser, as they are more precise, but each person should experiment with orbs in their own work, and observe what works best for them. It is not uncommon for orb preferences to change over time.

In all horoscope charts, aspects should also be calculated to the Ascendant and Midheaven. Traditionally, astrologers allowed one half of the amounts given in the table for each major aspect to the Midheaven and Ascendant, however, over time the preference appears to have shifted, and the common orb value tends to be used by many. While the meanings and values are the same as those given in the table, the traditional orb preferences were smaller due to the fact that these two positions are only sensitive points and have no power in themselves to form aspects. They are only capable of receiving aspects. Experimentation with aspects to these points in your own chart to observe how you are affected by them, and how the timing works for you will give a clearer indication of their functioning. Interpretation to the Ascendant is of primary importance in determining character and personality; and to the Midheaven in determining events. (Events, however, are also indicated by interpretation to the Ascendant.)

Another aspect, the Mundane Aspect, has been ignored by too many students of the science. Actually, there are two entirely different types of aspects known as Mundane, and they are not calculated by degrees but by houses. When two planets are two houses apart and about the same number of degrees from the cusp, they are said to be in mundane sextile; if three houses apart, in mundane square; if four houses apart, in mundane trine, etc. The true mundane aspect, however, is an entirely different matter, requiring detailed calculation of planet latitude. It is used only in advanced work, and while its nature is the same as that of the zodiacal aspect, it is undoubtedly of secondary importance. While very helpful for deeper interpretation of the horoscope, this is confusing for the beginner.

Another type of aspect is sometimes known as the Sign Aspect. Planets found in different signs but not within the orb for degree aspects may be in sign aspect to one another. It they are two signs apart, they are in zodiacal sign sextile; if three signs apart, in zodiacal sign squares, etc. However, these are of such minor importance that the student is again advised to postpone concern until later. They are mentioned here only to make the exposition complete. Focus on the aspects given, and when the student has become accustomed to how they function, introduce additional aspects for study.

During the stages of horoscope erection the aspects are normally noted on a graph called an **Aspectarian** found on most

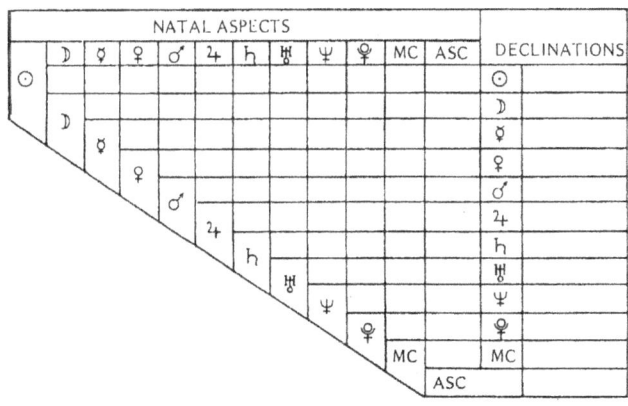

Figure 26. An aspectarian

chart paper. This is for convenience in later interpretation of the horoscope. One example of an aspectarian is given in Figure 26.

At this stage the student will do well to master the more limited astrological materials which he has already encountered, expanding his knowledge as ability and understanding broaden. Many volumes have been, and will be written on aspects. The information given above is regarded as basic, and its proper understanding is a secure foundation for further astrological development.

Review Questions for Chapter 8

1. Calculate the aspects between the following list of planets:

    Mercury 12° ♉ to Venus 11° ♋
    MC   29° ♏ to Jupiter 3° ♓
    Mars   8° ♉ to Saturn 5° ♒
    Uranus 4° ♉ to Moon 6° ♍
    Moon   1° ♑ to Jupiter 5° ♑
    ASC   29° ♓ to Sun 3° ♌
    Venus 23° ♎ to ASC 26° ♎
    Mars   2° ♏ to Pluto 28° ♋
    Saturn 3° ♒   to Sun 5° ♊
    Jupiter 15° ♌ to Pluto 15° ♎
    Moon   3° ♎ to Neptune 5° ♍
    Mars   24° ♊ to MC 22° ♐
    Uranus 21° ♈ to Neptune 20° ♍

2 List the steps to be followed in judging a horoscope.

3. Classify the above aspects as applying or separating and dexter or sinister.

4. Calculate the major aspects in your own horoscope.

REFERENCES:

1) Flavius Josephus, *The Antiquity of the Jews*, (Grand Rapids, MI: Kregel Publications, 1960), ch. 2, sec. 3, p. 27.

2) Josephus, op. cit. ch. 7, sec. 2, p. 32.

3) Strabo, Geography XVI.

4) Diodorus Siculus, *Library of History, Book I*

5) Egon Freidell, *A Cultural History of the Modern Age*.

6) *Aegyptiaca*, recorded by Panodorus (395-408 BCE).

7) Sepharial, *The New Manual of Astrology*, (Philadelphia, PA: David McKay, 1898), section on Hindu Astrology. Sepharial was the pen name used by Walter Gorn Old.

8) Shigeru Nakayama, *A History of Japanese Astronomy*, (Cambridge, MA: Harvard University Press, 1969). Very few references are cited in this chapter. Needless to say, this is just an introduction to the history of astrology and the student is urged to read standard works on the history of astrology.

9) *The New English Bible*, (New York: Oxford University Press, 1976), Book of Daniel, ch. 1, vs. 20; and ch. 2, vs. 10. The term Chaldean in the Old Testament referred to wise men, primarily astrologers and magicians.

10) Sepharial, *The Science of Foreknowledge*, (Mokelumne Hill, CA: Health Research Institute, facsimile reprint–1918).

11) Claudius Ptolemy, *Tetrabiblos;* (the author recommends the translation by Ashmand), translation by J.M. Ashmand, (Mokelumne Hill, CA: Health Research, 1917 – fascimile).

l2) Leopold Dukes, *Der Orient, IV*, (1843), p. 657.

13) Guido Bonatus, *De Astronomia*.

14) Michel de Nostredame, *The Complete Prophecies of Nostradamus*, (New York: Nostradamus, Inc, 1969).

15) Johann Wolfgang von Goethe, T*he Autobiography of My life: Truth and Poetry*, (New York: Wiley and Putnam, 1846-1847).

16) William Lilly, *An Introduction to Astrology*, (London: G. Bell and Sons, LTD, 1933).

17) Additional historical references about astrology are:

RH Allen, *Star Names and Their Meanings*, (New York: Stechect, 1899)

J. Burnett, *Earry Greek Philosophy*, (New York: World Publishing, 1930)

J.L.E. Dryer, *History of Planetary Systems from Thales to Kepler*. (Dover, New York, 1953)

M. Eves, *History of Mathematics*, (New York: Rinehart, 1969)

Cyril Fagan, *Astrological Origins*, (Chicago, IL: RR. Donnelley and Sons Co, 1973)

Cyril Fagan, *Zodiacs Old and New*, (London: Ascombe Press)

Manly Palmer Hall, *Story of Astrology*, (Boston, MA: Patronage House Publishers, 1975)

S.N. Kramer, *History Begins at Sumer*, (New York: Doubleday, 1959)

Jack Lindsay, *Origins of Astrology*, (New York: Barnes and Noble, 1971)

M.A. Murray, *The Splendor That Was Egypt*, (New York: Praeger, 1964)

E.N. Plunket, *Ancient Calendars and Constellations*, (London, J. Murray, 1903)

P. Wheelwright, *The Presocratics*, (New York: Odyssey Press, 1966)

18) For further information on astronomy see the following references:

Robert B. Culver, *Astronomy*, (New York: Barnes and Noble Books, 1979)

Morton Grosser, *The Discovery of Neptune*, (New York, Dover Publications, Inc., 1962)

Will Kyselka, and Ray Lanterman, *North Star to Southern Cross*, (Honolulu: The University Press of Hawaii, 1976)

W. M. Smart, Textbook of *Spherical Astronomy*, (Cambridge: Cambridge University Press, 1977)

19) The Celestial Equator is the projection into space of the Earth's equator.

20) Maurice Wemyss, *The Wheel of Life*, (London, L.N. Fowler and Co, LTD, 1927).

Maurice Wemyss is the pen name under which Scottish archaeologist Duncan McNaughton carried out his astrological research and writings.

21) For further information about planetoids and theoretical planets see the following references:

Charles E.O. Carter, *Here, There and Everywhere, Astrology*, Vol. 37, (UK: 1963)

Ivy Goldstein-Jacobson *The Dark Moon Lilith*, (Pasadena, CA: Jacobson, 196)

Charles Jayne, *The Unknown Planets*, (New York: Astrological Bureau, 1974)

John Robert Hawkins, *Transpluto or Should We Call Him Bacchus?* (Dallas, TX: Hawkins Enterprising Publications, 1976)

Roger Jacobson, T*he Language of Uranian Astrology*, (Franksville, WI: Uranian Publications, 1975)

Ludwig Rudolph, Wute-Lefeldt *Ruler for Planetary Pictures*, (Hamburg, Germany: 1974)

Wemyss, Maurice, *The Wheel of Life, Vol III*. (London: L.N. Fowler and Co., LTD, 1930)

22) For further information about the asteroid belt see the following references:

Eleanor Bach, *Ephemerides of the Asteroids Ceres, Pallas, Juno, Vesta 1900-2000*, (New York: Celestial Communications, 1973)

Zipporah O. Dobyns, PhD, *The Asteroid Ephemeris*, (Los Angeles, CA: TIA Publications, 1977)

Emma Belle Donath, *Asteroids in the Birth Chart*, (Tempe, AZ: AFA, 1976)

Esther Leinbach, *Planets and Asteroids*, (Seattle, WA: Vulcan Books, 1974)

H.C. Meier, *Ephemeride, Kosmobiologische Jahrbuch*, 1971 (Aalen, Germany: Ebertin–Verlag, 1972)

23) For the sake of convenience, the lumaniaries are called planets.

24) Some of the most commonly used ephemerides are:

The American Ephemeris, 1900-2000, compiled by Neil Michelsen, (San Diego, CA: Astro–Computing Services), Available in both noon and midnight; in yearly, 10 year segments, 50 year segments, and 100 year segments.

Concise Planetary Ephemeris, 1900-2050, (Medford, MA: Hieratic Publishing Co), available in both noon and midnight; 50 year segments.

The Rosicrucian Ephemeris 1900-2000 Oh TDT (Midnight), (Oceanside, CA: The Rosicrucian Fellowship, 1984). One of the rare volumes that contains the declinations for the planets on a daily basis.

Simplified Scientific Ephemeris, 1900-1999, (Oceanside, CA: Rosicrucian Fellowship), available in yearly and 10 year segments.

Raphael's Ephemeris, (London: W. Foulsham & Co, LTD) available in noon yearly segments.

The Astrolabe World Ephemeris 2001-2050 (Midnight) featuring longitudes and declinations for Sun, Moon, planets, Chiron and the asteroids. (Atglen, PA, Whitford Press) Aslo available in noon calculations.

25) Some of the most popular tables of houses are:

AFA Tables of Houses: Campanus, Koch, or Placidus Systems, (Tempe, AZ, AFA, 1977)

American Book of Tables, by Neil Michelsen, (San Diego, CA: Astro–Computing)

Table of Houses, International Edition, Oceanside, CA: Rosicrucian Fellowship, 1995)

26) Time at the longitude of zero degrees at Greenwich, England, is considered as Greenwich Mean Time and used in all calculations today.

27) Time change books available are:

Doris Chase Doane, *Time Changes in Canada and Mexico*. (Tempe, AZ: AFA. 1968)

Doris Chase Doane, *Time Changes in the USA*, (Tempe, AZ: AFA. 1973) Doris Chase Doane, *Time Changes in the World*, (Tempe. AZ: AFA, 1971)

Neil F. Michelsen. *The American Atlas*, (San Diego, CA: Astro-Computing Services, 1978)

28) *The part of Fortune in Astrology,* by Judith Hill, (Stellium Press, 2010)

29) *Astrology of the World Volume I: The Ptolemaic Inheritance,* by Benjamin Dykes, PhD, (Minneapolis, MN: The Cazimi Press, 2013)

www.ingramcontent.com/pod-product-compliance
Lightning Source LLC
Chambersburg PA
CBHW051131160426
43195CB00014B/2425